International Handbook of
Computer Security

International Handbook of
Computer Security

Jae K Shim, Ph.D

Professor of Business

California State University, Long Beach

GLOBAL
professional
publishing

This edition published by
Global Professional Publishing Limited
The European Innovation Centre
Fitzroy House
11 Chenies Street
London WC1E 7EY

ISBN: 978-0-85297-679-1

Typeset by Kevin O'Connor

Printed and bound in the United States by
International Book Technology

Contents

About the author

Jae K. Shim, Ph.D. is a professor of business at California State University, Long Beach and CEO of Delta Consulting Company, an IT consulting and training firm. Dr. Shim received his M.B.A. and Ph.D. degrees from the University of California at Berkeley (Haas School of Business). Dr. Shim has been a consultant to commercial and nonprofit organizations for over 30 years. Professor Shim has also published numerous articles in professional and academic journals. Dr. Shim has over 50 college and professional books to his credit, including:

The Vest-Pocket Guide to Information Technology (Wiley), *The International Handbook of Computer Networks* (Trentop Management Books), *The Artificial Intelligence Handbook: Business Applications in Accounting, Banking, Finance, Management, and Marketing* (Thompson-Southwestern), *The Manager's Handbook of Client/Server Computing in Business and Finance* (Thompson-Southwestern), *Database Management Systems: A Handbook for Managers and Their Advisors* (Thompson-Southwestern).

What This Book Will Do for You

International Handbook of Computer Security is written primarily to help business executives and information systems/computer professionals protect the computer and the data from a wide variety of threats. Computers are an integral part of everyday operations. Organizations are dependent upon their computer systems. A failure of the computer system is likely to have a critical impact on the organization. Potential vulnerabilities in a computer system could undermine operations and therefore, must be minimized or eliminated.

This book addresses a wide range of computer security issues. It is intended to provide practical and thorough guidance. The emphasis is on practical guidance rather than on theory. It helps managers improve computer security in their organizations.

Security concerns have heightened in the recent years. News events about computer related data errors, thefts, burglaries, fires, and sabotage dominate. The nature of the computing environment has changed significantly. The increased use of networked computers, including the Internet, Intranet, and Extranet, has had a profound effect on computer security. The greatest advantage of remote access via networks is convenience. This convenience makes the system more vulnerable to loss. As the number of points from which the computer can be accessed increases, so does the threat of attack. More caution is clearly needed to counter such threats. Weak computer security and lack of internal controls increases an organization's vulnerability.

The major steps in managing computer security are discussed in this book . We help business executives identify resources in their organizations that need to be protected. Sometime, the organization may not even consider the information to be "valuable" to anyone else and may not be willing to take security precautions. This is a serious mistake. Frequently, hackers are interested in obtaining access to private or confidential information. Hackers often steal or destroy data or information simply because it is there! Other hackers may delete or destroy files in an attempt to cover their illegal activity. The book highlights the need for a comprehensive security plan in an organization and explains why a casual attitude towards computer security is never justified.

The costs and benefits of various security safeguards are also discussed. The cost of a security safeguards includes not only the direct cost of the safeguards, such as equipment and installation costs, but also indirect costs such as employee morale and productivity. It is important to recognize that increasing security typically results in reduced convenience. For example, employees may resent the inconvenience that results from implementing security safeguards. Too much security can be just as detrimental as too little security; a balance must be maintained.

Special emphasis is given to contingency planning. Assuming that security is violated, how do you recover? What are the data backup policies? What are the legal consequences? What will be the financial impact? A risk analysis should be performed in planning computer security policies and financial support.

Computer security risks fall into one of three major categories: destruction, modification, and disclosure. Each of these may be further classified into intentional, unintentional and environmental attacks. The threat comes from computer criminals and disgruntled employees who intend to defraud, sabotage, and "hack". It also comes from computer users who are careless or negligent. Lastly, the threat comes from the environment; an organization must protect itself from disasters such as fire, flood, and earthquakes. An effective security plan must consider all three types of threats: intentional attacks, unintentional attacks, and environmental attacks.

Insurance is also discussed in the book. What is the company's degree of risk exposure? Insurance policies should be taken out to cover such risks as theft, fraud, intentional destruction, and forgery. Business interruption insurance covers lost profits during downtime.

This book addresses the security concerns of business managers. This book is designed as a practical, "how to" guide. We provide extensive examples to illustrate practical applications. The tools and techniques in this book can be adopted outright or modified to suit individual needs. Checklists, charts, graphs, diagrams, report forms, schedules, tables, exhibits, illustrations, and step-by-step instructions enhance the book 's practical use. Answers to commonly used questions are also given.

Chapter 1

Organizational Policy

Today the cost to businesses of stolen, misused, or altered information can be high, especially if real or purported damages to customers can be traced back to mismanagement. That's why you must value your information resources within the context of your business goals and constraints.

The objective of security management is to eliminate or minimize computer vulnerability to destruction, modification, or disclosure. Before we can discuss information security, we must see how that security works.

A key consideration is the physical location of the organization. Naturally, more security is needed in areas of high crime, although this may take the form of less expensive generic physical measures. Who uses the information will also affect the security measures chosen. Some users need to alter data; others simply need to access it.

If a security plan is to be effective, top management must be fully convinced of the need to take counteractive steps. To assess the seriousness of a computer breakdown or loss of data, each business has to evaluate threats to the company, the potential losses if the threats are realized, and the time and cost that will be necessary to recover from any breach in security.

The proliferation of networks scatters security issues across the globe and increases the need for inexpensive but effective levels of security. Physical security measures reflect the location of each component, but procedural measures, especially in a large organization, though they may seem obtrusive, are of equal importance.

Personal computers are another potential security threat. More and more people operate their PCs with telecommunications services to connect to central computers and network services. To limit the damage that can be done each user must be identified and that identity authenticated. The user is then allowed to perform only authorized actions.

Audits can be very valuable for detecting security violations and deterring future violations. A security violation may be indicated from customer or vendor complaints that show discrepancies or errors; on the other hand, variance allowances can cover up fraudulent activity.

Audit trails used to produce exception reports are especially valuable to managers. Standard questions include who accessed what data, whether the data were altered, or whether access-only employees attempted alteration. Exception reports are best used daily because they are after-the-fact reports. You may also choose to look only at reports from areas of high vulnerability or where there is a history of corruption or attempted corruption.

A good manager will know the types and forms of information generated and how the information is used by the business before planning how to manage it. Security measures in an information resource management program must be practical, flexible, and in tune with the needs of the business. A risk-management approach recognizes alternatives and decision choices at each step in information resources management in order to develop a program that meshes with ongoing business practices.

It is your responsibility as a manager to (1) assist with the design and implementation of security procedures and controls, and (2) ensure that these remain effective by continuous internal audits. To do this you must:

- Identify the risks.
- Evaluate the risks.
- Install appropriate controls.
- Prepare a contingency plan.
- Continually monitor those controls against the plan.

Misuse of information is costly. Ask yourself, "Where in the business scheme does this information work?" identifying not only the department but also the type of usage (strategic, tactical, operational, or historical). This will help you determine how secure that information must be. Its value must justify the expense of protecting business data. For instance, because encryption is relatively expensive, it's usually reserved for higher business use (strategic or tactical). Encryption software uses a fixed algorithm to manipulate plain text and an encryption key (a set of random data bits used as a starting point for application of the algorithm) to introduce variation. The machine instructions necessary to encrypt and decrypt data constitute system overhead. As a result, processing speed may be slowed. Operational business uses may use simpler controls such as passwords.

Security Administration

Security should be administered in the context of how the organization needs to control, use, and protect its information. Protection needs to be appropriate and reasonable given management's risk posture. Three levels of security (physical, procedural, and logical) used in tandem can reduce risk.

Physical Security

Physical security, the first in line of defense, is the one that usually comes to mind when you hear the word "security." This level literally separates those who are authorized to use certain types of information from those who are not. It also creates and maintains an environment in which the equipment is not exposed to damaging environment hazards like extreme heat or flooding, natural disasters, fire, power failure, or air conditioning failure.

Detection devices warn of an environmental failure, and automatic systems can protect against damages. Heat and smoke sensors and thermostats for temperature and humidity are standard equipment in computer centers. Attached to automatic shutoff devices, they protect your computer system should critical limits be exceeded. Some natural disasters cannot be foreseen, especially in the usually windowless domain of the computer center, but disruption of service can be kept to a minimum by using backup centers.

At backup centers themselves, physical security takes a heightened purpose. Your company may want to join a data center insurance group. The group data center should be able to handle the total workload of each member organization. During regular operations, the data center may be used by a third party.

Human control is more elusive. Traffic, especially at the beginning and end of the business day, can overburden card-access systems. The physical layout of the building and the routes employees use to reach their workplaces can also overburden checkpoints. Guards, usually low-paid, are susceptible to bribery and relaxation of standards. Additionally, during high traffic times there may not be enough guards to check employee ID badges, or register visitors.

Procedural Security

Daily users of information systems gain great insight into their workings. They can identify holes in the process. Employees generally know if their system is being audited (as they should, to discourage corruption); if they are not being audited, the temptation to tamper with the system may be too great to resist. Companies with high turnover are particularly susceptible to employee modifications of the system.

Careful hiring and processing of employees, then, is one way to instill procedural security. Threats from mentally unstable employees are obvious. However, without the proper safeguards all current and former employees have access to the company's computer resources. Among the proper safeguards:

◆ Revoke passwords as soon as an employee is terminated or if he is even suspected of infringement.

◆ Use lists of authorized personnel to control entrance into system.

◆ Constantly monitor logs generated by computer systems that report access to sensitive areas.

◆ All transactions processed should be reviewed and audited.

These actions constitute a fundamental level of control over business operations that lets the whole organization know that management is concerned with security and is devoting time and money to seeing that its security objectives are met.

Logical Security

Computer hardware or software should automatically control the people and programs trying to access computer resources. Data encryption is an example.

Generally, all three levels of security must be combined to form the right mix for a given element. This is called an access control system. Its goals are to:

◆ Prevent unauthorized physical or logical access to facilities or to information via electronic formats,

◆ Track user computing and telecommunication activities, and

◆ Establish a basis for, and then enforce, a set of authorizations for all persons and program attempting to use electronic information resources.

General Controls

General controls apply to all computer activities. General controls to prevent theft of equipment and data and to restrict access to the use of equipment and data are the primary consideration.

Security Software

The objective of security software is to control access to information system resources, such as program libraries, data files, and proprietary software. Security software identifies and authenticates users, controls access to information, and records and investigates security related events and data.

Establishing a Security Policy

Every organization should have a security policy that defines the limits of acceptable behavior and how the organization will respond to violations of such behavior. The policy assigns accountability and delegates authority across the organization. It will naturally differ from organization to organization, based on unique needs. Optional policies include:

◆ No playing of computer games on corporate computers.

◆ No visiting adult web sites using corporate Internet accounts or computers.

◆ An embargo against the use of specific protocol if it cannot be administered securely.

◆ A prohibition against taking copies of certain corporate electronic documents out of the office.

◆ No use of pirated software.

Questions you must answer include: How will violators be reprimanded or punished? Will organizations respond to violators inside the organization? Will it be different from the response to violators outside the organization? What civil or criminal actions might be taken against violators?

Security policy should not be set piecemeal. This leads to inefficiencies, holes, in the system, poor valuation of information elements, and inconsistencies. And it costs more to set policy piecemeal.

Publishing the policy is vital. The owners of information can best assign information elements to a particular classification. Top management is in the best position to evaluate consequences. About one percent of all business information should have the highest level (and therefore costliest) classification. Mid-range classifications typically have about 40 percent of all business information.

Policy statements set program goals, give detailed direction for carrying out procedures, and explain absolute requirements of the information security system. Policy statements should be concise and not require modification for at least five years; standards or procedures usually must be modified no more often than every three years.

Your security policy should be a broad statement that guides individuals and departments as they work to achieve certain goals. Specific actions needed to realize goals will be contained in supporting standards rather than in the policy document.

The security policy should be concise and to the point, generally not exceeding 10 pages. It should be easy to understand. It should emphasize the roles of individuals and departments. It is not the purpose of the security policy to educate individuals. That objective is better achieved through training.

The rationale for a security policy should be stated, explaining its purpose, including why data integrity must be maintained. Come down hard on the importance of maintaining the confidentiality and privacy of information resources. The organization must have information continuously available; any interruption can have serious financial consequences.

Computer security must be everyone's responsibility, so the computer security policy should encompass all locations of the company and all of its subsidiaries. Because security is only as strong as its weakest link, everyone in the organization must be held to the same set of standards. This means that the standards have to be flexible enough to be used in a wide variety of circumstances while remaining consistent across the organization.

The security policies apply to all data and computer facilities, including standalone computers, Internet and Intranet sites, local area networks (LANs), and wide area networks (WANs), as well as all forms of electronic communications, including email, fax, and data transmissions. They should also encompass relevant printed material, such as documentation and technical specifications.

Computer security is a means to an end, not an end in itself; it is an integral component of your organization's overall risk management strategy. It should therefore be evaluated periodically to respond to changes in technology or circumstances. Assign authority for issuing and amending the security policy to a committee such as the Information Technology Management Committee that must determine when circumstances justify departure from policy. All exceptions must have committee approval.

For a security policy to proceed, all individuals and departments must participate. It is well established that individuals are more likely to accept the security policy (or any other policy!) if they have had input during its creation, but the real benefit of employee participation is the knowledge they bring.

The relationship between the computer security policy and other corporate policies should be spelled out. For example, the computer security policy should be used in conjunction with the firm's policies for the internal control structure and contingency plans, including business interruption and resumption plans.

The policy should ensure compliance with all laws. Privacy and confidentiality issues have a serious effect on computer security. Increased governmental regulation is likely. The legal department should help department heads comply with the laws.

The responsibilities of the Information Systems department and its security personnel should be defined in the security policy document. These responsibilities might be to:

◆ Be responsible for all computer network and communications.

◆ Provide systems development methodology for security needs.

◆ Ensure that security personnel have the training and skills to perform their duties.

◆ Provide computer security assistance to other departments.

◆ Be responsible for all cryptographic methods and keys.

◆ Manage virus detection software for both networked and standalone computers.

◆ Acquire hardware or operating systems as needed.

◆ Authorize the use of networks.

◆ Review, evaluate, and approve all contracts related to information systems.

For personal computer systems, the security policy should address additional precautions; for instance:

◆ All original data should be backed up regularly.

◆ Virus detection software must always be used on PCs, especially before copying data or programs onto the network.

◆ Certain types of confidential or important data should never be stored on a local hard drive; instead such data should be stored on the network, or on floppy or compact disks or a removable hard drive, so that it may be stored in a secure place.

◆ PCs should not be directly connected to the Internet, since the Internet is a source of both virus infections and hackers. Internet access should be only through the company's Intranet server, which can protect itself.

Additional policy components can include the policies regarding the hiring, performance, and firing of information workers, though they should not be overly specific.

Security should be continuous in all situations, and not limited to protecting against intentional attacks. The board of directors should write a clear statement of security intention, including:

◆ Definitions of behaviors that will not be tolerated or that will result in disciplinary action or dismissal.

◆ Standards of protection necessary at every company location, and

◆ Allocation of responsibility to one person (ideally) or to a group, with the authority to carry out the policy, set budgets, and approve objectives.

The Security Administrator

The security administrator sets policy, subject to board approval. He also investigates, monitors, advises employees, counsels management, and acts as a technical specialist.

The security administrator establishes the minimal fixed requirements for information classification and the protection each classification needs in terms of physical, procedural, and logical security elements. He assigns responsibilities to job classifications and explains how to manage expectations to policy.

The security administrator advises other information security administrators and users on the selection and application of security measures, giving advice on how to mark (written and electronic "stamps") and handle processes, select software security packages, train security coordinators, and solve problems.

The security administrator investigates all computer security violations, advises senior management on matters of information resource control, consults on matters of information security, and provides technical consultation for business activities.

Finally...

Finding and keeping qualified employees requires a large cash outlay, especially when qualified individuals are scarce. Computer security will depend on how well those employees are supervised and motivated. One theory is that employees who know that their company values its security, reviews its practices, alters faulty programs, and punishes wayward employees as well as outsiders will be less likely to commit fraud and more likely to report it.

Security for system components should be commensurated with their value to the business. Total security is not possible; even attempting it would be prohibitively costly, as well as overly burdensome to users. Therefore, top management should be aware of the varying risks of computer information loss or modification. They should be part of the administrator function reporting directly to senior management.

Chapter 2

Physical Security and Data Preservation

The first line of defense for a computer system is to protect it physically: the plant, the equipment, and the personnel. Physical security protects the data, its integrity, accuracy, and privacy. An effective physical security system will prevent a security failure. However, should a system be successfully attacked, it should create an audit trail for investigators.

Computer equipment is at higher risk if it is easily accessible by the public or in a high crime area. And, of course, sometimes people authorized to be on your premises steal. The cost of theft can be very significant, far higher than the replacement price of the stolen equipment, because the company may also lose valuable data, especially if your work has not been properly backed up.

Computer Facilities

In the past, when computing tended to be centralized, it was easier to label a structure as the "computer center." With distributed computing, that is no longer possible. All areas where computing is done and from where an attack may be launched are vulnerable. Unauthorized access to computer facilities should be restricted through the use of surveillance equipment.

Facilities should be designed to protect computers, taking into account environmental factors like heating, cooling, dehumidifying, ventilating, lighting, and power systems. For example, the ducts of air conditioning units should be secured against access with heavy-gauge screens.

The following safeguards help protect computer facilities from both accidents and disasters like fire and floods:

◆ Adequate emergency lighting for safe evacuation in case of fire or other disaster.

◆ Fireproof containers to protect media (disks, tapes, or other output).

◆ User manuals for equipment and software to maintain continuity of proper operations.

◆ Surge protectors to protect the computer system against power line disturbances.

As computers become smaller, they can be housed in smaller areas and this changes the way facilities are designed. The layout of computer facilities is important in planning for computer security.

Central computer facilities should be housed near wire distribution centers but away from junctions of water or steam pipes. The room should be sealed tightly to minimize smoke or dust from outside.

Wire management is simple with multilevel computer racking furniture, which offers space flexibility and is available from several suppliers:

◆ Ergonomic Workstations Ltd. (*http://www.ergo-ws.com/*)

◆ Information Support Concepts (*http://www.iscdfw.com/*)

◆ LANSTAR (*http://lanstar.com/*)

◆ Page Concepts (*http://www.pagec.com/*)

◆ PC Innovations, Inc. (*http://www.pcinnov.com/*)

◆ Salix Group (*http://www.salixgroup.com/*)

◆ Stacking Systems, Inc. (*http://www.stackingsystems.com/*)

◆ Systems Manufacturing Corp. (*http://www.smcplus.com/*)

◆ Workstation Environments (*http://www.workenv.com/*)

Roll-out shelves may be used for quick access to servers. Security cabinets should be used for controlled access to critical hardware and server systems.

If wiring is a concern, cables can generally be run along the walls. Racking shelves generally contain multistage openings for improved access to cables with a wide range of plugs and cable connectors.

Aluminum channels or I-beams can be used to raise components and cabinets if there is danger of flooding. Placing network equipment next to processing equipment can save cabling costs. Smaller components may be stacked vertically to conserve floor space and reduce cable costs. The Salix Group, for example, offers Spectro Data for networks; it is not limited by layout size and can be used for high-capacity four-level configuration.

Multilevel units are cost-effective, and if they are ergonomically designed, productivity increases. The main work surface should provide vibration-free areas for screen, keyboard, and digitizing palette, with additional workspace for accessing other documents and equipment.

Americon (Stacking Systems, Inc.), for instance, offers server cabinetry for both active monitoring and closet environments. Its Network Solutions cabinetry may be used when floor space is at a premium. Its LAN Manager consoles allow for multiple stacking of servers, monitors, keyboards, and mice, along with desk surfaces and storage space. The LAN Commander cabinets contain these security features:

- Lock-in suspension glide shelving
- Seismic strapping for servers
- 180-degree rotating doors for access to both sides of the server
- Whisper-cool exhaust fans
- Heavy rated casters for moving from place to place
- Rear access through sliding doors

Optional accessories include:

- Remote access for consoles as far away as 250 feet
- Pullout server shelves
- EIA rack mounts for Ethernet equipment
- Induction fans for cooling when not on a raised floor

Workspace Resources (*http://www.workspace-resources.com*) provides design and marketing services for the office and contract furniture industry. It coordinates the needs of businesses with the capabilities of furniture manufacturers.

Environmental Considerations

Computer facilities are susceptible to damage from a variety of environmental factors:

- *Heat* can cause electronic components to fail. Air conditioning is generally essential for reliable operation. Take simple precautions to ensure that air can circulate freely. Backup power should be available to cool down the computer system even if the primary power fails.
- *Water* is an obvious enemy of computer hardware. Floods, rain, sprinkler system activity, burst pipes, etc., can do significant damage. Check that the water pipes are routed away from computer facilities. Instead of a traditional sprinkler system, consider using a less potentially harmful fire-extinguishing agent.
- *Humidity* at either extreme is harmful. High humidity can lead to condensation, which can corrode metal contacts or cause electrical shorts. Low humidity may permit the buildup of static electricity. The floors of computer facilities should either be bare or covered with anti-static carpeting. Monitor humidity continuously to keep it at acceptable levels.

◆ *Dust, dirt, and other foreign particles* can interfere with proper reading and writing on magnetic media, among other problems. Personnel should not be allowed to eat or drink around computers. The air should be filtered and the filters replaced regularly.

◆ *Power failure* can render all equipment useless. Brownouts and blackouts are the most visible sign of power failure. However, voltage spikes, which can cause serious damage, are much more common. Spikes like those produced by lightning may either damage equipment or randomly alter or destroy the data. A drop in line voltage can also lead to malfunction of computer equipment. Voltage regulators and line conditioners should be used if electricity fluctuates. Think about installing an uninterruptible power supply.

Maintenance and Preventive Care

Regular maintenance can help prevent the unexpected downtime that can be caused by the weather and other environmental factors. Run diagnostic programs as part of regular maintenance and keep a maintenance log. You can quickly identify recurring problems by scanning the logs. At a minimum, log the following information:

◆ Type of equipment serviced

◆ Manufacturer and identification number of equipment serviced

◆ Date of service

◆ Services performed, including the results of diagnostic tests

◆ A note indicating whether the service was scheduled or not

Computer areas should be kept cleaned and dusted, with no eating, drinking, or smoking allowed. Set up programs to train your personnel in proper handling of computer equipment, peripherals, magnetic media, and CD-ROMs, reminding them of basic things like not putting magnetic media near telephones, radios, or other electronic equipment, and writing labels before placing them on disks.

Set up a regular cleaning schedule for computer and peripheral equipment, and use cleaning products recommended by the manufacturer. Never spray electrical equipment directly with cleaning liquids. Clean keyboard surface with a damp cloth and vacuum with special computer vacuums.

Printers need to be cleaned to remove fibers, dust particles, and lint. Magnetic media devices, especially the read/write heads and transport rollers, can be cleaned with commercial products. Dust, smoke, fingerprints, and grease building up on recording surfaces can lead to crashes or permanent damage to the equipment and magnetic media.

Simple precautions, such as using static-resistant dust covers, can protect equipment, but never use them when equipment is in use or it may overheat.

Water Alert Systems

Water alert systems should be installed wherever water might damage computer equipment, generally in the basement or in floors above the computer systems. Water sensing systems, which are especially useful in protecting electrical cables under the floor, should be installed within suspended ceilings and inside water-cooled computer cabinets and process cooling equipment. The water sensors should activate both an alarm and a drainage pump.

Static Electricity

Static electricity results from an excess or deficiency of electrons. An individual can easily become charged to several thousands volts. While the current form electrostatic discharges are too low to harm humans, they can do a lot of damage to electronic equipment.

You can protect against electrostatic discharges by grounding, shielding, filtering, and limiting voltage. Vinyl flooring is generally better than carpeting to avoid static electricity buildup. Simple precautions can also minimize the dangers, such as:

◆ Using anti-static sprays
◆ Grounding computer equipment
◆ Using anti-static floor and table mats
◆ Maintaining a proper level of humidity

Humidity Control

Humidity should be tightly controlled. When air is too dry, static electricity is generated. When it is too high, above 80 percent, there may be problems with electric connections and a process similar to electroplating starts. Silver particles migrate from connectors onto copper circuits, thus destroying electrical efficiency. A similar process affects the gold particles used to bond chips to circuit boards. An optimal relative humidity level is 40 to 60 percent.

Wires and Cables

In distributed computing, it's essential to protect the wiring system. Generally there are two options for wires and cables, copper or optical fiber. While fiber optics offer significant performance and security advantages, they cost more to install. However, the cost disadvantage rapidly diminishes as the volume of data to be transferred increases.

Fiber optics work by sending light signals along very thin strands of glass or plastic fiber. The fiber's core is surrounded by cladding. The cladding causes the reflections, which guide the light through the fiber.

Two common types of fiber are multimode and singlemode. Multimode, which has a larger core, is used with LED sources for LANs. Singlemode fiber, which has a smaller core, is used with laser sources. Plastic optical fiber has a much larger core; it uses visible light.

Cables and wires are fragile. A buffer coating protects the fiber from damage. Additional protection is provided by an outer covering, the jacket.

It is not possible to repair damaged wires; they must be replaced. In the process, the electrical properties of cables may be affected, in turn affecting the reliability of the data. Establish alternate paths for cables that are critical.

Fiber optics are more secure than copper. It is relatively easy for someone to tap copper lines if they can obtain access to them at any point. Such wiretaps are very difficult to detect. In contrast, it is much harder and more expensive to tap optical fibers. Moreover, normal operations are disturbed by a fiber optics tap, which can therefore be detected more easily. Yet even with fiber optics, a skilled person with proper equipment might tap the system undetected, so though fiber optics provide a deterrent to crime, they are not perfectly secure. Of course, the best way to protect sensitive data is to use encryption.

Fiber optics are not affected by electric or magnetic interference. Copper wires have to be shielded with cabling and grounded metal conduits.

On the other hand, the ends of all fiber optic cables must be microscopically smooth. They have to be exactly aligned and positioned. This requires expensive special equipment and highly trained personnel.

An experienced person should certify any data wiring. The person should:

♦ Perform a visual inspection.

♦ Check that each cable is connected correctly.

♦ Check that there are no crossed pairs.

♦ Use a reflectometer to detect if there are any constrictions, bad terminations, or external interference.

Purchase orders for any wiring should specify:

♦ Who will certify the wiring.

♦ What equipment will be used to test the wiring.

♦ What standards will apply.

Protecting Information

The integrity, accuracy, and privacy of data are essential in any organization. Data lacks integrity if anything is:

◆ Missing

◆ Incomplete

◆ Inconsistent

◆ Poorly designed (in a database environment)

Data accuracy is not the same as data integrity. Data is accurate if

◆ It is reliable, and

◆ The data is what it purports to be.

Data privacy requires that only authorized individuals have access to data.

Destroying Data

Data that is no longer needed must be destroyed. Information on magnetic media is typically "destroyed" by overwriting on it. While this appears to destroy the information, there are many subtleties to consider. For example, if the new file is shorter than the old file, information may remain on magnetic media beyond the new file's end-of-file marker. Any information beyond that can be easily retrieved. Overwriting the entire medium is safer but time-consuming. Instead, use other methods, such as degaussing. Degaussing are essentially bulk erasure devices; when used within their specifications, they provide adequate protection.

Formatting a disk does not safely destroy all information. Magnetic media may retain a latent image of the preceding bit value after the writer insertion of a new bit value because it is not possible to completely saturate the magnetization. While normal read/write operations are not affected by this limitation, it does pose a security threat exploitable by anyone with sophisticated equipment.

Papers and other soft materials, such as microfiche and floppy disks, can be shredded. Some shredders cut in straight lines or strips; others cross-cut or produce particles. Some shredders disintegrate material by repeatedly cutting and passing it through a fine screen. Others may grind the material and make pulp out of it.

Burning is another way to destroy sensitive data. As with shredding, burning means that the storage medium can no longer be reused. Yet even with burning, you need to be careful. It's possible using special techniques, for example, to retrieve printed information from intact paper ashes, even though the information may no longer be visible to the human eye.

Controlling Access

Access controls guard against improper use of equipment, data files, and software. The oldest method of restricting physical access is with a lock. Locks are of two types, preset and programmable.

With *preset* locks, it's not possible to change the access requirements without physically modifying the locking mechanism. The combination on *programmable* locks, whether mechanical or electronic, can be more easily changed as security needs change, but their basic problem is that the entry codes are often easy for an observer to obtain. To overcome this problem, some electronic locks use a touch screen that randomly varies the digit locations for each user and restrict directional visibility to a perpendicular angle.

Make sure there's only one door for access premises into a secured access, and the entrance should not be directly from a public place. It should be self-closing and it shouldn't have a hold-open feature. A combination or programmable lock may be sufficient. Install an alarm system.

One development in access control combines security with asset management. For example, it's possible to link a laptop with a specific individual and detect when the asset is moved in, out, or within a facility.

Security guards and guard dogs can also be used to restrict access; their physical presence serves as a deterrent.

Pre-employment screening and bonding are essential when hiring security guards. Certain states, such as New York, have mandatory training requirements for guards.

The limitations of guards, however, are well-known. They can easily become bored with routine work and may not fulfill their duties as expected. It's easy for someone to forge identification to get past a guard. Through procedural error, guards may also allow unauthorized individuals access to restricted areas.

Dogs have excellent hearing and a keen sense of smell. Guard dogs can be trained to "hold" intruders until security personnel arrive. On the other hand, security dogs mean you'll need additional liability insurance and training and maintaining dogs is expensive. Finally, they generally cannot differentiate between authorized and unauthorized visitors.

Still, security is enhanced if guards or dogs patrol the facilities often at random intervals. This psychological deterrence lets a potential intruder know that he might be caught. A determined attacker, of course, is unlikely to be bothered by psychological deterrents, so guards and dogs should always be backed up through other means.

Something as simple as lights can greatly enhance security. Lights make it easier for security personnel to carry out surveillance. Lights also make it harder for intruders to enter the facilities. Lights may be left on all the time, put on timer or ambient control, activated by motion detectors, or manually operated.

To limit access, a security system must be able to discriminate between authorized and unauthorized individuals. The three general discrimination methods are:

◆ *Identification*, comparing the physical characteristics of an individual with previously stored information. Access depends on who the person is. It may verify the individual's signature, personnel number, code, voice print, palm print, fingerprint, teeth print, or other personal traits. Secondary authorization, such as the user's place of birth, may be required for highly sensitive information.

◆ *User's name plus passwords* based on some combination of letters or numbers. There should be no logic to the password, so it cannot be easily guessed. Access depends on what the person knows. Passwords should be changed regularly; inactive passwords (e.g., more than four months old) should be deleted. When an employee leaves, block his password immediately. If a user changes a password, you'll need controls to prevent use of the old password. Passwords should not be shared. Access control software allows a minimum password time period in which a new password cannot be changed or a new password matching an old one will be rejected.

◆ *Cards/keys.* Access can depend on what a person possesses: Cards, keys, badges, etc. Improper access may be signaled by an alarm. Evaluate any unauthorized access pattern. You might want to look into smart cards, in which the user enters both an identification number and a randomly generated code that changes each time it's used or at stated times.

Computer and terminal access controls include:

◆ *Automatic shut-off*: The system signs off the user if the user fails to sign off after a transmission is completed.

◆ *Call-back*: A phone call is made to the terminal site to verify the user's identity before access is granted.

◆ *Time lock*: Access is denied to the system during specified hours, such as after normal business hours.

Within the plant, areas containing sensitive data should be accessible only to authorized personnel. These areas, including the computer room, should have only a single entry door that can be operated by an encoded magnetic ID card or by physical controls, such as a librarian keeping a log. A lockout should result from repeated errors.

Your logs should be automatic; they should list the employee ID number, time of access, and function performed. Data dictionary software provides an automated log of access to software and file information. Use intrusion detection devices like cameras and motion detectors to monitor sensitive areas for the presence of unauthorized individuals.

Are your people diligently honoring the controls you've set up over processing, maintaining records, and file or software modification? Each individual function (e.g., accounts receivable, payroll) may require its own password so that users have access only to limited areas. The computer can keep an internal record of the data and time each file was last updated to compare against the log. The hour to access key files can be limited to prevent unauthorized access after normal working hours.

Files should be assigned different levels of confidentiality and security, such as Top Secret, Confidential, Internal Use Only, and Unrestricted. Confidential information should not be displayed on computer screens.

To control access to sensitive data, map access requirement to system components based on job function, with an appropriate segregation of duties. Temporary employees should be restricted to a specific project, activity, system, and time period. If you want to avoid possible data manipulation, don't give programmers free access to the computer area or the library. Keep those important disks locked up.

Hardware Security

While computer hardware has improved tremendously in reliability and speed, these technological advances have not always been good for computer security and data integrity.

Parity checks and data redundancies are critical for error-free data processing. Extra bits included at predetermined locations help catch certain types of errors when data is moved back and forth between different devices or from storage to registers.

◆ *Vertical redundancy checks (VRC)*, though common, have some problems. VRC are simple and inexpensive to implement. First, you determine whether there should be an odd or even number of "1" bits in each character's binary code. An error is detected if the correct number is not transmitted. The basic flaw with the approach is that two errors may offset each other, allowing the error to go unnoticed. Furthermore, there is no standardization on the use of odd or even parity.

◆ *Longitudinal redundancy checks (LRC)* provide an additional safeguard since VRC may not detect all the errors. This technique involves the use of an extra character generated after some predetermined number of data characters. The bits in the extra character provide parity for its row. LRC had its limitations. It cannot correct multiple errors or errors in ambiguous position (ambiguous bit is correct for VRC but incorrect for LRC), or errors that do not result in both VRC and LRC indication.

◆ *Cyclical redundancy checks (CRC)* are typically used when extra assurance of the accuracy of data is needed. A large number of redundant data bits if used, which requires longer transmission times and extra space in memory. The primary advantage of this technique is that any single error, whether in data bit or parity bit, would be detected.

Hardware typically has several features to protect the data during input, output, and processing.

◆ *Dual-Read* reads the same data twice and compares the two results. Any discrepancy indicates an error.

◆ *Read-After-Write* reads the data immediately after it's recorded to verify to verify the accuracy of the write function.

◆ *Echo Check* is used to verify the reception of a signal when the data is transmitted to another computer or to peripheral devices such as printers.

◆ *Replication* is an important feature for critical applications. A backup computer/ site is used in case of failure of the primary computer. Fault-tolerant or fail-safe computers contain at least two processors that operate simultaneously; if one fails, the other processors pick up the load. When a critical application requires extensive communication facilities, the back up equipment should contain both communication equipment and a processor. Repairs or replacement of malfunctioning equipment should be immediate.

◆ *Overflow* may result when an arithmetic operation, such as dividing by zero, results in values beyond a computer's allowable range. This function is typically built into the computer hardware.

◆ *Interrupts* are generated when the hardware detects deviations in order to maintain the integrity of the data processing system. For example, input/output (I/O) interrupts result when a previously busy device becomes available. The equipment then checks after each I/O interrupt to determine if the data has been written or read without error. I/O interrupts are generated when the Escape or Enter key is pressed. From a security perspective, interrupts can affect logs or cause the execution of unauthorized programs. Other types of interrupts include program check, machine check, and external. *Program check* interrupts terminate the program as a result of improper instructions or data. *Machine check* interrupts are generated by defective circuit modules, open drive doors, and parity errors. *External* interrupts result from pressing an Interrupt key, from signal from another computer, or from timer action. From a security perspective, for example, the built-in electronic clock in the processor can be used to generate an interrupt at a specified interval to ensure that sensitive jobs do not remain on the computer long enough to be manipulated. Plan for the possibility of loss of data so that it does not result because of interrupts.

Most integrated circuit chips on hardware equipment are inscrutable to a lay person. There are hundreds of thousands of transistors on a small semiconductor. Still, it's possible for a bug to be planted into electronic equipment, and it may be very difficult to detect. Several techniques may be used to seal hardware against such tampering.

Keep records of hardware failure and computer down times. Schedule regular maintenance, and record the results. If computer equipment needs frequent servicing, personnel might be tempted to bypass controls and take shortcuts, raising the possibility of human errors considerably. Analyze your records for unfavorable trends in downtime or frequently unscheduled service calls.

The hardware inventory logs for all computer equipment and peripherals should contain at least the following information:

◆ Description of the hardware

◆ Manufacturer's name

◆ Model number

◆ Serial number

◆ Company identification number

◆ Date of purchase

◆ Name, address, and phone number for the source of the item, whether store or manufacturer

◆ Date warranty expires

◆ Department or location where the hardware equipment will be used

◆ Name and title of individual responsible for the equipment

◆ Signature of the responsible individual or department head

◆ If the equipment is taken off premises, the date and time the equipment is checked out, and the date and time it's returned, along with the signature of the authorized individual.

Hardware inventory logs should be stored in a secure location with a copy stored off-site. All hardware should be etched or engraved with the company name, address, telephone number, manufacturer's serial number, and company's identification number. To prevent theft, locking devices should secure computer equipment and peripherals to desktops, etc.

Software and Devices for Physical Security

A wide variety of software and devices is available to prevent computer theft. Computer Security Products, Inc. (*http://www.computersecurity.com*) provides an excellent assortment.

CompuTrace Theft Recovery Software

CompuTrace Theft Recovery Software is primarily for laptop computers, but it may be used with desktops. Once the software is installed, it works silently and transparently. Regularly and often, it uses the computer's modem to place a toll-free call to a monitoring center after checking to see if the modem is attached and in use. It turns off the modem speaker when making its scheduled call. The computer's serial number and the origination telephone number are recorded with each call.

If the computer is stolen, you call CompuTrace's theft hot line to activate the Theft Recovery Assistance Procedure. The next time the stolen computer's modem dials in to the monitoring center, CompuTrace acquires the origination telephone number and determines its location. Local law enforcement authorities are then notified.

CompuTrace is available for DOS and Windows-based systems. It cannot be deleted; it even survives a hard-drive format. The only way to delete it is to use a registered copy of the uninstall disk.

CompuTrace, which uses less than 7K of memory is not detectable by antivirus software and does not appear in any directory. It's fully automated and does not interfere with other applications.

It works form any phone line in North America. It works even if the phone number is unlisted. It doesn't rely on Caller-ID technology. It even works from hotel and office phones that require you to dial a prefix to reach an outside line. If CompuTrace doesn't detect a dial tone when it first calls out, it will try again with various prefix combinations.

Though CompuTrace's default calling schedule is usually 5 to 7 days, you may change it. It's also possible to program the computer to call with greater frequency once it has been reported stolen. If the modem is not connected or is in use at the scheduled call time, CompuTrace keeps on trying periodically until the modem is available.

As an added benefit, CompuTrace may be used to manage computer assets in large organizations. The CompuTrace Monitoring Center provides up-to-the-minute listings of all computers and their locations. It's easy to determine whether the computer is in a regional office, at an employee's home, or on the road. Monitoring reports can be downloaded from a private web site. Reports can be distributed via email or fax. CompuTrace is available from Computer Security Products, Inc. (800-466-7636).

PC and Peripheral Security

Most computer equipment and peripherals can be quickly secured with steel cables, an easy and inexpensive theft deterrent. Special fasteners protect RAM chips and internal components. Cover locks can be used to:

◆ Lock the computer case

◆ Block access to disk drive slots

◆ Block access to CD-ROM

◆ Block access to the on/off switch

The base of the cover lock can be attached to most flat surfaces. The locks may be keyed alike or differently. Master keying is also possible.

Lock-down plates provide additional security. The Cavalier Security System, for example, consists of two steel plates. The base plate contains the lock and is secured to a table. The insert or top plate is attached to the equipment to be protected. The plates come in various sizes depending on the width and length of the equipment to be secured. By selecting a size slightly smaller than the equipment's footprint, the lock-down plates appear less obtrusive.

Network Alarm

EtherLock Alarm System (*www.computersecurity.com*), which plugs into the hub, allows you to use your network as an alarm system. It interfaces with your existing alarm and uses the network's wiring to secure computers; an alarm is triggered if a network wire is unplugged. It does not affect system performance or network throughput.

LockSoft Remote Management Software for EtherLock systems (*www.computersecurity.com/etherlock/locksoft.htm*) allows for control of the EtherLock system from any computer on the network. A central monitoring site can be notified of the attempted theft. Running LockSoft software with EtherLock lets you perform the following tasks from the central console:

◆ Receive network-based alarm reports when computers are disconnected.

◆ View the connection status of all protected devices.

◆ Remove individual devices from the protection loop for maintenance or relocation.

◆ Arm, disarm, and test all EtherLock systems connected to the network.

◆ Allow password-protected access to secure individual computers. This feature lets administrators give notebook users the flexibility to disconnect their machines.

At the time of this writing the cost of EtherLock 10T Base Unit was $1948. The base unit can hold up to 16 Protection Modules, each costing $799 and supporting up to 12 devices. Therefore, the full system can protect up to 192 computers and peripherals on a single hub. Its modular design allows for expansion as the LAN grows. The minimum configuration requires one protection module.

The LockSoft software that comes with EtherLock computer security is available for Windows and DOS-based systems. Administrator software is included; it collects data on the EtherLock systems and the devices being protected.

To protect laptop computers, the NoteLock security bracket ($19.95) may be used in conjunction with the EtherLock security system. You can connect to or disconnect from the network using an Ethernet cable. The LockSoft program simply

22

asks you to enter a personal password. Personnel can be alerted if an attempt is made to remove a secured laptop computer form the network. Logging off from the network or powering down the computer does not affect the security features; only the appropriate password can be used to disconnect the laptop from the network.

The SimmLock security bracket ($19.95) is designed to protect memory chips (SIMMs), microprocessors, hard drives, and other internal components. Security personnel are alerted if any attempt is made to remove the computer case or access its internal components. SimmLock brackets can be affixed to monitors, external hard drives, and other peripheral equipment not directly connected to the network.

Asset Tracking

Tamper-proof asset-tracking security tags should be affixed on computers and peripherals. STOP (Security Tracking of Office Products) asset tags are available from Computer Security Products, Inc. (http://www.computersecurity.com/stop/index.html). Security plates or tags help in three ways: (1) they deter theft: a thief is less likely to steal tagged equipment; (2) they help in recovering stolen equipment; and (3) you can use these tags for asset management.

STOP plates link equipment data to a worldwide tracking and retrieval service. If equipment is lost or stolen, law enforcement authorities can be notified to track it. The barcode on STOP tags can be used to track equipment day to day and can interface with the Microsoft Access database.

The STOP security plate, made of photo-anodized aluminum, is secured to equipment using cyanoacrylate adhesive. It takes about 800 pounds of pressure to remove the security plate. If the plate is removed, the equipment casing will be noticeably altered.

Behind each plate is an indelible tattoo, "Stolen Property," that is chemically etched into the equipment. If someone succeeds in removing the security plate using special tools, the indelible marking is exposed, as are the company identification number (optional) and a toll-free number for verification and anti-theft information. This tattoo cannot be removed without defacing the case. Defacing is recognized by police and equipment sellers as a sign that the property is stolen.

Each security plate bears a warning that the property is monitored and traceable. It also warns that a tattoo has been etched into the equipment. Each plate also has a barcode to tack information and a toll-free telephone number to call in case lost or stolen equipment is found.

Once equipment is registered, the STOP retrieval service will oversee its return. In any case of theft, STOP will help register the loss with law enforcement agencies in the United States and abroad.

STOP's hand-held barcode scanner, along with its asset tracking software, helps you maintain the inventory of valuable equipment. Inventory records are updated simply by scanning tags. The software will report on missing or out-of-plate hardware. It can also report on mobile equipment by registering who borrowed the equipment and when it was due.

The software is network-ready and customizable. It's based on the Microsoft Access database, but the software includes a runtime module, so Microsoft Access is not required to use the software. Source code is available for you to customize it.

Each STOP security plate costs $25. Quantity discounts can significantly reduce the cost of each plate. For example, if 10 or more plates are ordered, the price drops to $15 each. If more than 500 plates are ordered, the security plates cost less then $9 each. The Tattoo Activating Gel costs $2.50 for up to 10 security plates. For customized plates, the minimum order is 200 units and requires a one-time setup charge of $250.

The price of the security plate includes unlimited use for three years of STOP's anti-theft and retrieval hotlines and its recovery service.

After the first three years, unlimited use of these services costs $1 per year per machine, or $4 lifetime per machine. For large sites, a $200 flat fee per year covers an unlimited number of machines.

The STOP asset tracking management software costs $200 but is provided free with an order for 500 or more security plates.

The Intermec hand-held barcode scanner package costs $2,500 and includes:

- ◆ Communications dock and cable
- ◆ Charger
- ◆ Light wand and cord
- ◆ Power supply
- ◆ Barcode creation software
- ◆ STOP Asset Tracking Software

The Xyloc System

Xyloc access cards may be used to secure desktop computers and laptops. The cards automatically lock the computer and blank the screen when the authorized user with the card leaves a pre-defined area. They also automatically unlock the computer system when the authorized user returns with the card. The computer's session work is preserved when the computer is locked. Background tasks continue to run even when the system is locked.

The pre-defined area, the "active zone," can be set from one to 50 feet. It allows access by many users to a single computer. Communication between the access cars and the lock is encrypted to prevent an attacker from grabbing the code to create a clone. The system can be programmed to deploy incrementally to individual PCs, to workgroups, or enterprise-wide.

The Xyloc system is suitable when you need high security and restricted access to the computer system and system files. The system works either alone using the access card or, for even greater security, in conjunction with a password. On a LAN, it's possible to remotely manage several Xyloc systems from a central facility. The software maintains the audit trail and logs events. The information may be used, for example, to determine if proper security procedures are being followed.

The Xyloc key contains a low-power radio transceiver (short for *transmitter-receiver*) with a unique user identification code. It's powered by a lithium battery that typically lasts from six months to a year. A battery meter lets you know how much power remains. The Xyloc Card Key is compatible with other ID and security badges. There's an encrypted channel for all communications with the lock.

The lock is a small device containing a low-powered transceiver. The lock simply plugs into the keyboard, serial, or USB port; it's powered by the port and contains a built-in status light.

The Xyloc Access Card System consists of two pieces of hardware and software for the access control card. Each package includes one card key, one lock, and software. Additional pieces are available separately.

Card Technology

Many manufacturers are combining multiple technologies, such as bar codes, magnetic strips, proximity, and smart cards, on a single card. Such a card may also serve as a photo ID, which in effect gives it an additional function. A universal reader device that can support multiple formats will be required.

Current access control technology typically works by keeping doors locked. It denies access to everyone except those who can show or do something to get through the door. Technology is now proceeding in a new direction. Doors are left open, closing only when an unauthorized person tries to enter. For example, users might carry cards with chips that would tell the door that the person is an authorized user and that it's okay to stay open. The approach of anyone not carrying the appropriate card would close the doors.

There are potential problems associated with this technology. For example, assume a group of four people approaches. Only three of the four are authorized. The system should be capable of stopping the group and letting only the authorized individuals through.

Software for access control systems can help in collecting and managing a wide variety of data, which that could help determine, for example, the total amount of time spent on site by each cardholder. Access control data may be used to determine which employees are still in the facility during an emergency. This may save lives by helping authorities determine who might be trapped inside.

Visual Surveillance

Video surveillance is becoming increasingly popular. Cameras are more affordable. Image quality has improved tremendously. The components are getting smaller and more reliable. Cameras are more functional and responsive. Features such as panning, tilting, and zooming are common.

Digital videos, digital transmission of data, and digital storage are likely to increase the use of surveillance equipment. Digital storage allows security personnel to retrieve specific scenes quickly. Image quality tends to be much better than ordinary videotape.

Digital technology makes it possible to record and view images at the same time. Improvements in transmission media may mean that cameras at remote sites will replace more security officers. Remote monitoring and recording is becoming more feasible because of price deceases in components, including chips and memory.

Biometric Devices

Biometrics for access control purposes is on the horizon. It hasn't gained widespread popularity primarily because of its cost and lack of accuracy. Both are likely to diminish with improvements in computer processing. A facial recognition system for door access will soon be widely available. Companies are working on integrating fingerprint sensor technology into keyboards in order to restrict access to a terminal or a network. Miniature cameras at computer workstations may control access through facial recognition technology.

Chapter 3
Hardware Security

Software security depends on hardware security. If the hardware can be stolen or surreptitiously replaced, secure software will not help. Before the invention of the personal computer, computer machines called mainframes were so huge and bulky that they took up an entire room. To secure these machines, IT managers locked up the rooms. Now laptop and palmtop computers are small and portable, making it easier for these machines to be stolen. Companies use computers for various tasks such as storing sensitive information, doing online transactions, and accessing private and public networks. IT managers looking to protect their investments must consider securing the perimeter and allowing only authorized users access to their computers.

Some of the most common hardware problems are:

◆ Equipment and removable media can be stolen or replaced
◆ Security can be circumvented by changing hardware setup parameters
◆ Systems can be booted by unauthorized users or unauthorized software
◆ Boot media can be re-written by unauthorized software
◆ Unauthorized software can be executed from removable media

Some of the safeguards that can be taken are:

◆ Locking doors and securing equipment
◆ Having lockable cases, keyboards, and removable media drives
◆ Having a key or password-protected configuration and setup
◆ Requiring a password to boot
◆ Requiring a password to mount removable media
◆ Using read-only media
◆ Storing removable media in secured areas

Organizations that store and transmit sensitive and valuable information over both public and private networks should be concerned with information security. Unauthorized users can easily gain access to the unsecured, networked environment. For example, security breach can occur if the hardware, software, network connections, and authentication procedures are not protected with a security solution. In the past, the solution for information security may have resulted in locking a mainframe safely in a room with limited access. Today securing information is more difficult due to personal computers, the availability of high speed, inexpensive modems, and the popularity of the Internet. Attacks are becoming more sophisticated. Hackers have also gained sophisticated tools to automate attacks.

Information Week Research's ninth annual 2006 Global Security Survey (www.informationweek.com) conducted in partnership with Accenture in May and June, shows across-the-board threats to business computing environments. Fifty-seven percent of U.S. companies surveyed report being hit by viruses in the past year, 34% by worms, and 18% by denial-of-service attacks. Network attacks and ID theft were experienced by 9% and 8% respectively. It's no wonder that 48% of the 2,193 security professionals and business technology managers who completed the survey say managing the complexity of security is their top challenge.

Security technologies used	Security management
Antivirus 96%	◆ Security is about 6 to 8% of the IT budget in developed countries
Virtual private networks 86%	◆ 63% currently have or plan to establish in the next two years the position of chief security officer or chief information security officer.
Intrusion detection systems 85%	
Content filtering/monitoring 77%	
Public-key infrastructure 45%	◆ 40% have a chief privacy officer, and another 6% intend to appoint one within the next two years.
Smart cards 43%	
Biometrics 19%	◆ 39% acknowledged that their systems had been compromised in some way within the past year.
	◆ 24% have cyber risk insurance, and another 5% intend to acquire such coverage.

Figure 1: How large companies are protecting themselves from cybercrime.

*Source: 2006 Global Security Survey, **Information Week***

Security breach costs companies millions of dollars in losses, increased staff-hours, decrease in productivity, loss of credibility in the marketplace, legal liability, etc. Protecting sensitive and valuable information with both hardware and software solutions is critical to securing any company's future.

Physical Security

Physical security is almost everything that happens before a user (or an attacker) starts typing commands on the keyboard. Surprisingly, many organizations do not consider physical security to be of the utmost concern. It is one of the most frequently forgotten forms of security because the issues that physical security encompasses – the threats, practices, and protections available – are different for practically every different site.

When planning for physical security, several measures can be taken to protect the computing system and sensitive data as follows:

- ◆ Access control should only be given to users that require access to the specified data.
- ◆ Computer rooms should be evaluated on whether windows require bars or electronic detection devices.
- ◆ Access to rooms containing computers should be restricted except to specifically authorized personnel. These rooms can also be controlled with locked doors, posted guards, and other approved restraints.
- ◆ Protect computers with lockable equipment enclosures, lockable power switches, fasteners, and securing devices.
- ◆ Make sure that computers will operate in the environment that contains emanations from other electronic devices and that the computers will not interfere with other electronic devices.
- ◆ Keep the computer in a comfortable environment to prolong its life and ensure the safety of stored data.
- ◆ Shield the computer from sudden surges or drops in electrical line voltage by using surge processors or uninterruptible power supplies.

Data Integrity

In computer security, data integrity is as important to protect as the actual hardware equipment. Data integrity refers to the validity of data. If compromised, it makes the point of protecting your data useless. Data integrity can be compromised in a number of ways:

- ◆ Human errors when data is entered
- ◆ Errors that occur when data is transmitted from one computer to another
- ◆ Software bugs or viruses
- ◆ Hardware malfunctions, such as disk crashes
- ◆ Natural disasters, such as fires and floods

To minimize the threats of data integrity, consider the following options:

◆ Backing up data regularly

◆ Controlling access to data via security mechanisms

◆ Designing user interfaces that prevent the input of invalid data

◆ Using error detection and correction software when transmitting data

Network Backup

Recovering from a computer disaster can be very costly and time consuming, especially if a backup plan has not been implemented. In a world where intruders can come from both inside and outside, IT managers need a contingency plan to make sure that if an intruder wipes or sabotages an entire system they will be able to bring the data back. A critical procedure that should be in place in all corporations is backing up computer data to a network backup server. Having a centralized backup location can save you and your employees time and money from having to search for the backup tapes. For many organizations that support heterogeneous clients, they also need to consider a backup solution that provides this capability.

Retrospect Remote 3.0 from Dantz Development Corp. is a full-featured backup server. With the Remote Pack 1.0 client software, it can back up Windows and Macintosh clients to a dedicated Macintosh. Retrospect, running on a dedicated Macintosh, handles all backup, restore, duplication, and backup server tasks. Client sources can be hard drives, external or removable media, and files in subdirectories in the Windows environment or folders in the Mac environment. Retrospect provides a robust and flexible multiplatform network-client backup solution. A backup solution from Retrospect provides an easy and secure way to backup files.

Access Control System

To protect your data from intruders, consider securing the perimeter of your building. By allowing only authorized users access to your facility, you can greatly reduce the risk of someone walking into your building and stealing proprietary information. RAND, a well-respected, non-profit policy research organization, has made a provision to controlling physical security by means of staff access cards, alarms, surveillance cameras, and a proprietary facility guard force. Surveillance cameras record all entrances to and exits from the building, including the entire parking lot. The facility security guard force screens and signs in visitors, and conducts interior and perimeter patrols of the facility. The security guards respond to and investigate incidents and complaints and if requested, escort staff to their cars in the parking lot. Only RAND staff members are allowed into the facility. Entrance into the building is controlled by security guards and by electronically controlled card readers. Visitors must show identification, sign in, and be escorted by a RAND contact before they are allowed to come into the building.

Memory Data Integrity Checking

Ensuring the integrity of data stored in memory is an easy way to make sure your data is secured before it is ever saved to floppy disk or on the network. Companies should consider buying computers that use data integrity checking to prevent errors later on. If the computer is to play a critical role such as a server, then the computer with an error correction code (ECC) capable memory controller is an appropriate choice.

The two primary methods to ensure the integrity of data stored in memory are parity and ECC. Parity has been the most common method used to date, adding 1 additional bit to every 8 bits (1 byte) of data. The parity method has its limitation because it can detect an error but not perform any correction. On the other hand, error correction code is a more comprehensive method of data integrity checking that can detect and correct 1-bit errors. With ECC, 1-bit error correction usually takes place without the user even knowing an error has occurred. Kingston, an independent memory manufacturer, sells memory products that has data integrity checking for use in workstations, servers, desktops, portables, and printers.

Deploying a Security System

When planning a security system, you should form a strategy for your defense mechanism rather than randomly deploying gizmos. Three strategies to consider include perimeter security, interior security, and physical protection of individual assets. While you want to keep intruders out, you also want to limit the amount of damage they can do once they are inside.

Perimeter Security

Figure 2. ADT card reader

Source: ADT

Perimeter security means considering protecting the easiest points of entry for criminals, in most cases that would be doors and windows. Windows can be protected with small, easily mounted, devices that can sense when the glass has been broken and sound an alarm. Access control systems are complex, high-tech information networks but they are essential to office security.

Authorization can take many forms, including entering a code into a keypad, sliding a card through a scanner, or pressing a button on a wireless remote control. ADT, an electronic security company, sells access control systems such as a card reader to secure entry on doors (see Figure 2). These devices can help companies track the comings and goings of their employees.

Interior Security

Figure 3. Deltavision designer mount camera

Source: Deltavision

Interior security is as much a part of deterring intruders as it is about catching them in the act. Motion detectors can be used to set off alarms. A surveillance system such as cameras can deter

theft when they are placed in a location that can catch the intruder's eye. Deltavision, a Canadian CCTV manufacturer, sells a wall or ceiling mounted camera that interfaces with Deltavision recorders for 24-hour real time surveillance (see Figure 3). For other companies that worry about espionage, they can buy covert cameras that are disguised as clocks, telephones, or even exit signs.

Physical Protection of Individual Assets

Many computing devices are now small enough to be put in a briefcase and carried away. Cable kits can be an inexpensive solution to this problem. Some hardware devices can be connected to computers and set to trigger an alarm. Software can be installed in a laptop to let police track down stolen laptops.

Figure 4. PIX Firewall Series

Source: Cisco Systems Inc.

Integrated Hardware/Software Firewall Appliance

Firewalls have traditionally provided perimeter security by maintaining careful control of all connections between connected network segments. For IT managers looking for a dedicated firewall appliance that delivers strong security without impacting network performance, Cisco Systems Inc., the worldwide leader in networking for the Internet, provides PIX Firewall Series (see Figure 4). The Cisco PIX Firewall series delivers strong security in an integrated hardware/software appliance. The PIX Firewalls protect your internal network from the outside world by providing full firewall security protection. Its real-time embedded system enhances the security of the Cisco PIX Firewall series. Unlike typical CPU-intensive full-time proxy servers that perform extensive processing on each data packet at the application level, Cisco PIX Firewalls use a non-UNIX, secure, real-time, embedded system. It delivers superior performance of up to 256,000 simultaneous connections, over 6,500 connections per second, and nearly 170 megabits per second (Mbps) throughput. This level of performance is dramatically greater than that delivered by other appliance-like firewalls or those based on general-purpose operating systems.

The heart of the Cisco PIX Firewall series' high performance is a protection scheme based on the adaptive security algorithm (ASA), which effectively protects access to the internal host network by comparing inbound and outbound packets to entries in a table. Access is permitted only if an appropriate connection exists to validate passage. Another performance feature is cut-through proxy, which enhances authentication. Cut-through proxy challenges a user initially at the application layer, but once the user is authenticated and policy is checked, the PIX Firewall shifts session flow to a lower layer for dramatically faster performance. The PIX Firewall allows you to accommodate thousands of users without affecting end-user performance.

Total VPN Solution

Companies rely on virtual private networks (VPN) to allow telecommuters, customers, suppliers, and branch offices access to their internal information, as discussed in the next chapter (Software Security). Unfortunately, VPN security software requires extensive encrypting and decrypting on the server end, which means that users will experience performance degradation. As your organization grows and more people use VPN, the host computer will be further impeded in performance. Chrysalis-ITS, Inc., the provider of high-performance security solutions for the network security industry, has developed a hardware solution called Luna VPN. Luna VPN extends the security network connections across the Intranet, Extranet, and Internet by maximizing performance and security. It combines the security software and hardware acceleration into one package to provide a total VPN solution. With the Luna VPN hardware component, the encryption and decryption processing is offloaded from the host computer so that network throughput performance can be increased. By offloading this processing to Luna VPN, bottlenecks can be removed.

Chrysalis-ITS ran extensive tests on Windows NT and Solaris host systems and found that Luna VPN significantly increases the network throughput performance. For both Windows NT and Solaris, the tests were run using the software alone and with the Luna VPN. As shown in Figure 5, the card and software combination increases performance by up to eleven times for DES operations. For Triple-DES operations, adding the card to the software increases performance by up to nineteen times.

Figure 5. Luna VPN Network Throughput Performance

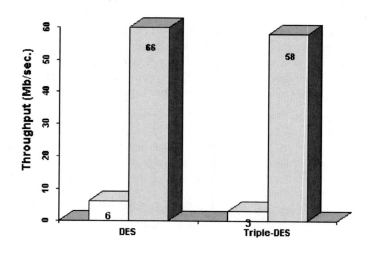

Source: A Security Assurance White Paper from Chrysalis-ITS

Chrysalis-ITS has also determined that processor overhead can be decreased when Luna VPN is added. Results from Chrysalis-ITS shows that adding Luna VPN to VPN software can significantly offload the host CPU. Moreover, adding a second processor to either Solaris or Windows NT systems does not offload processing from host processor as effectively as Luna VPN.

The combination of Luna VPN and VPN security software increases the flexibility, scalability, and centralized management of software with the performance, security and offloaded processing of hardware. This combination provides the following benefits:

◆ Enables up to 900% more throughput

◆ Removes processing bottlenecks from the host computer

◆ Provides scalability for thousands of users

Security Becomes a Priority

Computer theft and network break-ins are a growing concern for notebook users and their companies. Major computer vendors are dealing with these issues by offering security products to safeguard users' machines.

These major vendors include:

◆ IBM – offers Smart Card Security Kit, both smart card and a four digit PIN, on notebook's hard drive

◆ HP – offers smart cards on its OmniBook notebooks, Vectra desktop PCs and Kayak workstations

◆ Dell – offers a hard drive password feature on Latitude notebooks, OptiPlex desktops and Precision workstations

◆ Compaq – uses Fingerprint Identification Technology (biometrics instead of passwords) to log on to a network on its Deskpro, Armada, and Professional Workstation systems

Smart-card technology offers numerous security advantages to the corporation, including the following:

◆ Users can log-in from any PC on the network, enabling "roaming" between PCs and easy import of temporary or flex-time personnel

◆ A "digital signature" on the card provides instant proof of sender identity and message authentication

◆ Permanent encryption keys ensure that stored information is transmitted easily without compromising confidentiality

◆ Chip circuitry containing smart-card "intelligence" is tamper-proof, becoming void upon exposure to light

◆ Sensitive information is stored on the card itself, unlike biometrics user-authentication solutions, which store data within a system database, where it has the potential to be accessed illegally

◆ Smart cards can display an employee's identification photograph and double as a swipe card, providing the holder with access to company buildings and other facilities

Using Tokens for Dual-Factor Security

To gain access to a supposedly secure system for a sophisticated hacker or a determined insider does not take much if your confidential resources are protected only with a user password. Single-factor identification such as a password is not enough. Security Dynamics Technologies Inc. in Bedford, Mass., has developed the SecurID token for a two-factor identification. Factor one is something secret that only the user knows such as a Personal Identification Number (PIN) or a password. The second factor is something the user possesses such as the SecurID token. A token is a small device the size of a credit card that displays a constantly changing ID code.

Figure 6. SecurID token

Source: Security Dynamics

Carried by authorized system users, SecurID token, as shown in Figure 6, is a microprocessor-based handheld device that generates unique, one-time, unpredictable access codes every 60 seconds. To gain access to a protected resource, a user must enter a user name and a personal identification number, followed by the current code displayed on the SecurID token. The security server compares the password entered by the user with the proper password for that time period. The tokens require no card readers or time-consuming challenge/response procedures.

Some of the advantages of SecurID token are:

◆ Having an easy, one-step process for positive user authentication

◆ Preventing unauthorized access to information resources

◆ Authenticating users at network, system, application or transaction level

◆ Generating unpredictable, one-time only access codes that automatically change every 60 seconds

◆ Not requiring a token reader; can be used from any PC, laptop or workstation — ideal for remote access and Virtual Private Networks

◆ Working seamlessly with WebID for secure Web access

◆ Working across access control modules (ACMs) for multiple platform enterprise security

◆ Being tamperproof

Practical Examples: Tokens Used for Clinical Data Access

Securing sensitive data is especially important when it involves access to clinical data. Beth Israel Deaconess Medical Center in Boston uses the SecurID token from Security Dynamics to provide a single form of user authentication to a Web-based interface to the hospitals' medical databases. When Boston's Beth Israel Hospital and Deaconess Medical Center merged in October 1996, the SecurID token helped them consolidate authorization access into a single form. The SecurID token gave them a single way to get on both systems with an identical look and feel. Beth Israel stores its patient records in a custom-built Mumps-based system, while

Deaconess uses a Sybase clinical-data repository. The new CareWeb interface saves the merged hospitals time and money.

The hospitals have looked at other security tools like biometrics but they dislike the fact that the hardware would have to be deployed on every PC. They were concerned with error rates caused by greasy fingertips, which could lock a medical worker out of access to urgently needed medical data. The SecurID token also provides interoperability with Cisco Systems Inc. and Intel Networking Systems Inc. routing products that made them compatible with virtual private networks (VPNs). Some users may be sending authentication passwords remotely over public networks.

The hospitals are now looking at smart cards to consolidate applications in the medical center. The medical center's environment includes swipe cards, digital certificates, VPN, and tokens.

What is a Smart Card?

A smart card is a credit card-sized device that has an embedded microprocessor, a small amount of memory, and an interface that allows it to communicate with a workstation or network. According to the Smart Card Industry Association, some 1.6 billion smart cards were issued in 1998. By 2005, that number is expected to triple to 4.8 billion cards. The most common application is the phone card, a smart card that stores a set value for use in public pay phones (see Table 1). By 2006, the second most common use of smart cards will be for identify/access applications. This projection reflects the growing confidence security suppliers and their customers have in the technology.

Table 1. Smart Card Applications and Growth Rates by Units Deployed

Application Cards Issued	In Cards Issued		Industrial Average
Smart Card Applications	**1997 (millions)**	**2006 (millions)**	**Growth Rate (%)**
Pay Phone	605	1,754	29
Global System for Mobile Communications (GSM)	20	50	25
Health Care	70	120	14
Banking	40	250	105
Identity/Access	20	300	280
Transportation	15	200	247
Pay TV	15	75	80
Gaming	5	200	780
Metering/Vending	10	80	140
Retail/Loyalty	5	75	280

Source: Smart Card Industry Association

Smart cards are valued for the security they offer especially in providing authentication. With smart cards, passwords and IDs are securely encrypted on the card. When combined with biometric finger-scanning technologies, users can even skip the PIN code. The broad appeal in corporate environments is the flexibility and multi-functionality of smart cards. A smart card can be personalized for each user. For example, a company using smart cards to provide access to network services could store each employee's network privileges and preferred system settings on his or her card. The employee could then access the appropriate servers and files from any terminal with a card reader, and the desktop would be customized with the employee's preferences.

Two characteristics make smart cards especially well suited for applications in which security-sensitive or personal data is involved:

1. The onboard processor can service requests from the network and return the results without divulging the sensitive data. For example, a smart card could be used to digitally sign data without divulging the user's private key.

2. The user can carry the data with him or her on the smart card rather than entrusting it to network storage because smart cards are portable. For example, a smart card could be used to carry personal information about the user such as medical records or digital certificates.

Microsoft Windows NT 4.0, Windows 95 and Windows 98 all support smart cards and smart card readers based on specifications established by the Personal Computer Smart Card (PC/SC) Workgroup, an industry group of leading PC and smart card companies. Smart card solutions that are Windows-compatible can be used with Internet Explorer to authenticate a secure connection and Outlook Express or Outlook 98 for sending and receiving secure e-mail.

Through the use of public key cryptography and X.509 certificates, smart cards securely store private keys, as well as public key certificates. An embedded private key is the digital certification representation of a user's identity. Smart card technology is key to digitally signed and encrypted messages, provides access to protected Intranet sites, and is a possible enabler to a single network sign on.

Two-Factor Authentication

Figure 7. SecurID 1100 smart card

Source: Security Dynamics Technologies Inc.

Security Dynamics Technologies Inc. offers two-factor authentication technology in a smart card version to ease their use on corporate intranets. Security Dynamics has already marketed two-factor authentication with the SecurID token. Its design of two-factor authentication is the same, involving a personal identification number (PIN) and a unique password. Its smart card version called the SecurID 100 Smart Card, however, will generate the unique password automatically and transmit it to the server without any user involvement (see Figure 7). For example, the same smart card could be used to gain access to the company's building, or store value on the card for use in the company cafeteria and vending machines.

With the SecurID 1100 smart card, organizations can customize the features to provide access to the physical building by incorporating magnetic stripes or holograms. The SecurID 1100 smart card can serve as a single form factor that can be combined with corporate employee badge systems and other security applications. It also provides other features such as electronic-purse applications that work in the corporate cafeteria, airlines or car rental companies. Other applications can be integrated with the smart card to develop custom applications for a particular environment.

Using Smart Cards in Banks

Guarding the privacy of their customers requires the strongest possible security for banks. One company that believes smart cards can provide this high-level of protection is the Union Bank of Switzerland (UBS), the third largest bank in the world. As of March 2003, UBS has deployed 12,500 smart cards among its employees, increasing at a rate of about 1,000 per month. Employees use the smart cards to gain access to the company network and files. Eventually, UBS plans to deploy smart cards to all 35,000 of its Swiss employees.

UBS' network is decentralized; therefore, it did not fit well with server-based authentication solutions. Smart cards, however, provide the ideal solution because they allow for authentication and a single sign-on (SSO). Schumann Security Software Inc., (www.scchumannsoftware.com) offers the Secure Single Sign-On (SAM/ SSSO) to deliver strong authentication and confidential data transfer. Unlike other systems, SAM/SSSO is a decentralized approach that does not require a central authentication server. The application uses DES encryption and RSA-based public key infrastructure (PKI) to provide strong, secure authentication. The General Security Service (GSS) API provides the common interface between the smart card and the secured applications. In cases where strong authentication has not been added to an application, the smart card also supports conventional login via a script engine that automatically logs on with a user ID and password stored on the smart card.

Figure 8. UBS' Smart Card Single Sign-On

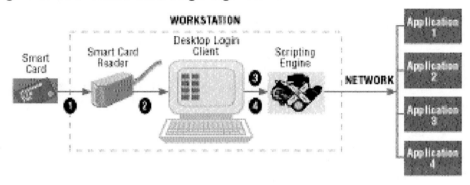

Source: Information Security Magazine, 1999

The basic components of SAM/SSSO are a smart card and a smart card reader. User logins and passwords are stored on a tamper-proof smart card and are only accessible using a single sign-on PIN. The smart card system is capable for off-site use while retaining on-site levels of security. With SAM/SSO, hours of wasted productivity changing or losing passwords can be avoided.

As shown in Figure 8, UBS' smart card single sign-on process starts when the user enters the smart card into the smart card reader and enters his or her ID and password. When authenticated, the user gains access to a graphical user interface (GUI) of available desktop applications. The user can then click on the desired application, triggering the scripting engine to launch the application script. The scripts can reside on either the user workstation or network server. The script delivers the appropriate ID and password from the smart card to the application logon screen.

While UBS' employees currently use the smart card system, bank customers could also use it to access back-office applications. The proprietary nature of its smart card system, however, will limit its appeal among clients. Standards must be in place in order to overcome the various customer-oriented smart card applications.

Smart Card Vulnerabilities

In computer security, smart cards can be used for access control, e-commerce, authentication, privacy protection, and a variety of other applications. While the flexibility of smart cards gives them many uses for businesses, it can also be susceptible to attacks. IT managers should consider the following vulnerabilities of smart cards before considering deployment:

◆ Attacks by the terminal against the cardholder or data owner
◆ Attacks by the cardholder against the terminal

◆ Attacks by the cardholder against the data owner
◆ Attacks by the cardholder against the issuer
◆ Attacks by the cardholder against the software manufacturer
◆ Attacks by the terminal owner against the issuer
◆ Attacks by the issuer against the cardholder
◆ Attacks by the manufacturer against the data owner

IT managers can prevent attacks of smart cards mentioned above if they use both a smart card and a portable smart card reader from one vendor. Cylink Corporation, a provider of encryption-based network security solutions, provides an advanced public key smart card called PrivateCard and a smart card reader called PrivateSafe. Cylink is an ISO 9001 certified company that provides security solutions to Fortune 500 companies. By using the smart card/smart card reader combination, users will be assured that their sensitive information is kept secured and their private information never leaves the smart card.

Figure 9. PrivateCard Smart Card

Source: Cylink Corporation

PrivateCard is an isolated tamper-proof smart card with an on-board microprocessor and control program (see Figure 9). The user's digital signature public and private key pair is produced on the card and never leaves the PrivateCard. Since all sensitive, private key cryptographic functions are performed securely on the smart card chip, it protects the private key from attacks and prevents the exposure to a potentially hostile external environment. PrivateCard can be integrated with other security products.

PrivateCard includes the following features:

◆ **RSA key generation** – supports up to 1,024 bit RSA functions

◆ **Random number generation** – numbers are randomly generated inside the smart card chip itself

◆ **RSA private key functions** – all private operations such as decrypt and digital signatures are performed on-chip

◆ **Support for multi-application and multi-data storage** – multiple keys and data objects may be stored on the card

◆ **Access control and PIN management** – provides a mechanism to ensure that PIN verification and access to keys or any data stored on files are performed securely by authorized users

◆ **PIN control** – includes the ability to change passwords after a specified period

◆ **Multiple-level file system** – allows information to be secured by directory

PrivateSafe is a smart card reader that fits between the keyboard and the PC to validate a user's PIN (see Figure 10). Since it connects between the keyboard and the PC, no additional hardware or external power supply is required. PrivateSafe isolates the user's private information on the smart card so that it never reaches the PC by passing keyboard input for other applications. It generates the public key pairs right on the PrivateCard so that the user's private key is never exposed to the PC.

Figure 10. PrivateSafe Smart Card Reader

Source: Cylink Corporation

What is eToken?

In security systems, a token is a small device the size of a credit card that displays a constantly changing ID code. A user first enters a password and then the card displays an ID that can be used to log into a network. As an alternative to entering an ID code from a token or deploying a smart card reader, Aladdin Knowledge Systems, an information security company, has developed the first USB-based device called eToken (see Figure 11). eToken is a car key-sized authentication token that plugs into a computer's Universal Serial Bus (USB) port, a standard feature on virtually all PCs and laptops manufactured since 1997. USB provides true "plug and play" for up to 127 peripherals. With USB, Aladdin seizes the opportunity to create a small key that would fit unobtrusively on an ordinary key chain and flexible enough to hold the information without an expensive reader. Containing its own processor chip, eToken can encrypt information, store private keys, passwords, digital certificates, and digital cash; and provide two-factor authentication for secure access to VPNs, remote access servers, subscription-based Web content and back-office applications.

Companies that require the need for convenient, remote access and protection from unauthorized users can no longer rely on conventional password schemes. Only two-factor authentication provides a high-level of security. Aladdin's eToken patent-pending technology opens and guards doors in e-commerce, e-banking, virtual private networks (VPNs), extranets, and WANs. It can protect sensitive data and resources by performing file encryption and access control functions. It can also sign or encrypt electronic messages so that they cannot be forged, changed or intercepted.

Aladdin's eToken provides the following features:

- ◆ **Easy to use** - No additional software or hardware is needed. The user inserts eToken into the USB port on a desktop, laptop, monitor or keyboard and types his or her password.

- ◆ **Cost-effective** - Costs between $20 or $50 per token, depending on the size of the setup.

- ◆ **Compact and convenient** – Only the size of a house key, eToken is portable.

- ◆ **Highly secure** - Security credentials are stored in a tamper-proof container, providing a higher degree of security than software-only solutions.

- ◆ **Versatile** – eToken can be used with many diverse applications and can contain a large number of private keys for different applications.

Figure 11. Aladdin's eToken

Source: Aladdin Knowledge Systems

What is Biometrics?

User authentication is the cornerstone of information security. Traditionally, people get access to secure places by using passwords or smart cards. A third method of user authentication is biometrics, identifying people based on their unique physical characteristics or behavioral traits. Biometrics uses a person's body features such as fingerprints, eyes and faces, and ways of doing things such as speaking and writing signatures to distinguish that person from all others. The catalyst for biometrics is the growing realization that passwords do not ensure computer and network security. Passwords can get lost, misplaced, forgotten, or written on notes and stuck on computer monitors for anyone to use. Valuable corporate data are often compromised as a result.

Compared with other security products, biometric technology has not gained wide acceptance. From the $100 billion spent on private security, Mentis Corp., a market research firm in Durham, N.C., says that the biometric market will total $100 million this year. With only a tiny fraction, Mentis predicts that the market will grow from 27% to 65% through 2000 as pattern-recognition software improves, computers become better able to handle biometric applications, and prices fall. As of today, this technology is still expensive and it is not as effective as other security products. Moreover, people are resistant to the idea of having their eyeballs scanned and see it as an invasion of privacy. The public's view of biometrics as intrusive is due to the fear of a Big Brother-like agency keeping tabs on fingerprints and voiceprints. Once they understand the limited nature of the data, however, they will become more comfortable with the technology and their perception will change.

Biometric products can come in a range of shapes and sizes. Some of the commercially available body identification methods include:

◆ **Voiceprint** – created by sound waves generated by an individual speaking a given phrase or password

◆ **Fingerprints** – ridges on fingers are converted to a digital template that can be compared with database records or a person

◆ **Palm prints** – measures the ridges of the palm and compares with a database

◆ **Hand geometry** – measures the size and shape of the hand

◆ **Hand veins** – scans the vein pattern on the back of the hand, creating a digital template that can be matched against stored patterns

◆ **Handwriting acoustic emissions** – analyzes sounds generated when a person signs his or her name

◆ **Iris** – video image of the colored portion of the eye is mapped by computer, creating a digital code based upon the individual pattern of the iris

◆ **Facial thermographs** – uses an infrared camera to capture heat emission patterns, producing a unique signature when heat passes through the facial tissue

◆ **Facial identification** – converts a video image of the face to a digital template, which can then be compared with a recorded image

The term "biometrics product" also has multiple definitions:

◆ A component that captures a human characteristic

◆ Associated hardware

◆ Application software

◆ Image matching software

◆ A standalone product

◆ A complete solution

◆ A platform or environment that supports biometrics authentication

Table 2. Common biometric techniques and how they rate

	User Criteria		System Criteria	
	Effectiveness	**Effort**	**Accuracy**	**Cost**
Dynamic signature verification	Excellent	Fair	Fair	Excellent
Face geometry	Good	Good	Fair	Good
Finger scan	Fair	Good	Good	Good
Hand geometry	Fair	Good	Fair	Fair
Passive iris scan	Poor	Excellent	Excellent	Poor
Retina scan	Poor	Poor	Very good	Fair
Voice print	Very good	Poor	Fair	Very good

Source: International Biometric Group, New York

Generally, biometric authentication is a two-phase process. The first phase involves scanning the user's personal characteristics such as their fingerprints, irises, faces, signatures, or voiceprints into the computer. Key features are then extracted and converted to unique templates, which are stored as encrypted numerical data in the computer's database. In order to get authenticated, the user must enter the second phase. In the second phase, the user presents his or her personal characteristic and the computer compares this information with the templates in the database. In the real world, matches will rarely be perfect due to extraneous factors and background interference.

Voiceprint

VoiceGuardian from Keyware Technologies, provider of Layered Biometric Verification solutions, is a two-step process of enrollment and verification (see Figure 12). The enrollment process consists of repeating a passphrase three times. An example would be "My voice is my password." Depending on the

Figure 12. VoiceGuardian

Source: Keyware Technologies

application, the voiceprint may be stored on the security server, smart card, or local PC. The second stage of verification is accomplished by speaking the passphrase one time. Once the passphrase is spoken, the live voice sample is evaluated with the stored voiceprint. At this point, the user is either allowed or denied access. If accepted, the user is allowed to access the secure resources.

In order to get accurate voice characteristics associated with the individual, the server uses a verification engine to provide physical authentication. Authentication

47

is performed through analysis of an individual's speech patterns at the phoneme level looking for the points of inflection and articulation, which form a unique voice pattern. This analysis provides the basis for the comparison with the individual's voiceprint stored in the database. The accuracy of voiceprint currently is only fair, although users do not consider voiceprint as intrusive.

Figure 13. Compaq Fingerprint Identification Technology

Source: Compaq Computer Corporation

Fingerprint

Fingerprint technology is based upon the fact that an individual's fingerprints have unique characteristics such as whorls, arches, loops, ridge endings, and ridge bifurcations. Verification systems capture the flat image of a finger and perform one-to-one verification. This verification is performed in a few seconds. Compaq Computer Corporation, supplier of personal computers, simplifies the login process with the Fingerprint Identification Technology, which is a biometric security product that replaces passwords with unique fingerprints (see Figure 13). Compaq claims that up to 50 percent of calls to corporate help desks are related to forgotten or expiring passwords. Furthermore, passwords represent potential security risks because they can be duplicated, forged or stolen. Fingerprint Identification Technology is a fingerprint reader that captures an image of the fingerprint and uses software algorithm technologies to convert the image into a unique "map" of minutiae points. The Compaq fingerprint reader makes two connections to your PC: one attaches between the keyboard and the PC, and the other attaches to the parallel port.

Compaq Fingerprint Technology uses minutiae-based processing for identification of an individual's finger. Minutiae points are unique data points that describe the fingerprint. This map of minutiae points, rather than the actual fingerprint, is encrypted and stored within the network (see Figure 14). A fingerprint can always be described by these minutiae points, but you cannot describe the minutiae points by a fingerprint. Since you cannot recreate the fingerprint from the data, your fingerprints image is never stored anywhere on the network.

Figure 14. Minutiae Points

  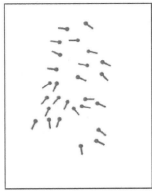

| Finger Image | Finger Image + Minutiae | Minutiae |

Source: Compaq Computer Corporation

An authorized user only has to register his or her minutiae points once to the server to serve as a digital record for this individual. Once the user's fingerprint is registered, the user only has to place the registered finger on the fingerprint reader attached to his or her PC to get logged on to the network. Since no user password is required, Fingerprint Identification Technology can improve network security. It is compatible with both Windows 95 and Window NT Workstation 4.0. For Windows 95 users, it gives them more security by preventing someone from bypassing the login by pressing "Esc" and gaining access to the operating system. Only after their fingerprint is authenticated will they be able to log on to the network.

Since fingerprints are unique, not easily copied, and relatively inexpensive, they are more likely to have widespread use. Authentication problems that plague computing might lead to an explosion in demand for such a security product as fingerprint scanning. Fingerprints can be used in a wide range of applications such as the Internet, electronic commerce, credit card, and ATM authentication. Once the cost of biometrics systems comes down enough and standards mature, passwords may well become a thing of the past for some people.

Iris Recognition

Iris recognition technology involves the use of a camera to capture an image of the iris, the colored portion of the eye. Your iris is one of a kind. An individual's right and left iris patterns are completely different. Each iris contains more than 266 measurable discriminators versus a fingerprint, which contains about 35 measurable characteristics (see Figure 15). As an internal organ, the iris remains stable, protected, and virtually unchanged from 18 months of age until death.

Two types of iris recognition systems exist today: active and passive. The active system requires participation on the part of the user because the system needs to be manually focused and the user must be close to the camera. The price of the active iris scan is several thousand dollars, including the camera hardware and the PC loaded with the software necessary to run the application. The passive system, however, is substantially easier to use because it incorporates a set of cameras to automatically locate the user's face and eye, removing the need to manually focus the camera. Passive iris scan is the most expensive biometric technology costing tens of thousands of dollars because this technology has only been available for a few years and it has not been mass produced.

Figure 15. Iris Identification

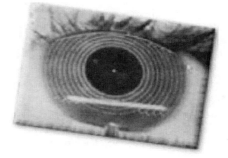

Source: Sensar Inc.

Figure 16. Iris

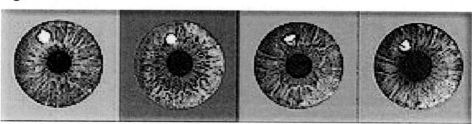

Source: Sensar Inc.

One of the issues why both active and passive iris scan technologies have not been used widely is the concern of privacy. Although the biometric identifier such as iris offers the convenience of not having to carry a photo ID and various cards, keys and codes, some people worry that we are moving toward a world where our personal privacy is the price of convenience. The public considers iris scan technology intrusive because the camera is taking a picture of one's eye. People are reluctant to divulge their personal information, thinking that the government in some way might use this information.

Figure 17. Iris Identification System

Source: Sensar Inc.

Sensar Inc. has developed a passive iris scan called the Sensar Iris Identification System that uses three video cameras to get a high quality image of the iris from as far away as three feet. This system automatically locates the user's face and focuses the camera without requiring the user to manually focus the camera. It maps the iris and converts it into a digital bar code, all in less than two seconds. The system consists of two modules: Identification Optical Platform and Identification Processing Platform connected by cable up to 10 feet in length (see Figure 17). Sensar claims that the matching probability of the Iris Identification System is greater than that of DNA testing.

Bank United, the largest bank headquartered in Texas, is the first bank in the United States to introduce Iris Recognition Automated Teller Machines (ATMs). Thousands of consumers in Houston, Dallas and Fort Worth will be able to withdraw cash from their accounts at the ATM just by looking at it. The customer only has to stand and look at the ATM. The camera will instantly photograph the customer's iris. If the customer's iris data matches the record stored at the time of enrollment, access will be granted. At the ATM, positive identification can be read through glasses, contact lenses, and most sunglasses. As more people rely on iris recognition and as the prices fall, we will see more use of the iris scan technology, especially in computer security.

Face Recognition

Your face is yours alone. Securing your computer network through face recognition makes it easy to unlock access to your company's applications and data. Miros Inc. in Wellesley, MA, (www.micros.com) provides TrueFace Network (see Figure 18), which incorporates neural network face recognition technology with TrueFace Isolator, the first automated neural network face locator.

Selecting a Biometric System

Many applications of biometrics are in use today. Before deciding on using biometrics in your organization, review the following steps from the Biometrics Consortium (www.biometrics.org):

1. Identify the level of security in the current application

    There are five basic parameters to be measured and valued:

    1. Total elapsed time taken for enrolling a person in the application.

    2. Total elapsed time taken by an individual to successfully use the application for a transaction.

    3. Percentage of false rejections of people using the application.

    4. Percentage of false acceptances of people who should not have been allowed into the application.

    5. Uniformity of performance of the application across the population who will use the application.

2. What improvements are required in the future application?

    For each of the above five parameters, define the target figures for the new application.

3. Find and select a biometric and manufacturer

    Lists of reputable manufacturers of all types of biometrics are available from the Biometrics Consortium.

4. Perform a screening test

    A "black box" test to see how well the biometric device performs relative to the parameters defined for the application. An independent biometric consultant or one of your employees should run the test.

5. Implementation of a biometric in an application

    The final step involves detailed integration, implementation, planning, and testing of the biometric within the overall application.

Questions to consider in a biometric system:

◆ *Biometric Type*

✓ How suitable is the biometric to the application?

✓ Are there any individuals or groups of people who cannot use the biometric?

◆ *Biometric Device*

✓ Is the price of the biometric device likely to fit the potential budget?

✓ Is the size of the biometric device significant?

◆ *Biometric Manufacturer*

✓ How is the reliability, quality of service, and reputation of the manufacturer?

✓ Who are the major clients of the manufacturer?

◆ *Fraud*

✓ Can the application be defeated if the criminal learns as much about the application as the developer knows and the biometric device as the manufacturer?

✓ If the biometric is used for verification, can the token be forged easily?

Remote Access Security Solution

Banks of modems have typically provided users remote access to corporate networks by dialing via the public switched telephone network (PSTN). This model is expensive in terms of equipment, support costs, and the cost of telecommunications service. With the Internet, companies can dramatically reduce their remote access costs by implementing VPN technology. The use of VPNs can foster business-to-business integration that enables electronic commerce over the Internet.

Extending your network to the outside world raises the question of how to protect your network security and data integrity. Contivity™ Extranet Switch 2600 from Nortel Networks intends to meet the challenge by providing secure extranets for business partners and secure connectivity for remote users (see Figure 19). Contivity™ Extranet Switch 2600 offers industrial-strength remote access to corporate travelers and trading partners. It also provides the functionality, performance, and security for a secured extranet.

Figure 18 Contivity™ Extranet Switch 2006

Source: Nortel Networks

Contivity™ Extranet Switch 2006 provides the following features and benefits:

◆ **Cost effective** – allows you to leverage the cost by using the Internet as the network infrastructure to provide a secure extranet at both the central site and branch office

◆ **Flexible and ease of use** – designed as a "plug and play" device, allowing it to work with existing network infrastructure components such as routers, firewalls, and authentication servers

◆ **High performance** – designed with all the necessary hardware and software to support VPN tunnels, encryption, compression, and filters for up to 200 simultaneous active users

◆ **Flexible security** – provides integrated, flexible security architecture to ensure that only authorized users can access the network

◆ **Standards-based technology** – supports constantly changing VPN and extranet technology standards

◆ **High availability** – allows up to 2000 simultaneous users

◆ **Flexible management** – fully configurable from any browser using HyperText Markup Language (HTML) and Java configuration and monitoring

◆ **Broad client support** – supports industry-standard PPTP clients from Microsoft and third parties

Contivity™ Extranet Switch 2006 supports leading Certificate Authorities (such as Entrust), Radius providers (such as Bay Secure Access Control, Funk, and Merit), and Token providers (such as Security Dynamics, AXENT, Secure Computing, and LeeMah Datacom) to allow customers easy incorporation of their extranet into their existing security infrastructure. It can use either its internal Lightweight Directory Access Protocol (LDAP) server or an external LDAP server such as Netscape Directory Server to authenticate and differentiate between users.

Contivity™ Extranet Switch 2006 supports the following standards:

◆ **Tunneling** – supports Point-to-Point Tunneling Protocol (PPTP), Layer 2 Forwarding (L2F), Layer 2 Tunneling Protocol (L2TP), and IPSec. *Note:*

Tunneling is a technology that enables one network to send its data via another network's connections.

◆ **Authentication** – supports LDAP, RADIUS, Windows NT, Security Dynamics, and AXENT

◆ **Encryption** – Ron's Code 4 (RC4), Data Encryption Standard (DES), and Triple DES

Intrusion Detection System

Many network security products such as firewalls and authentication systems provide critical security functionality, but they offer limited visibility in the network data stream. Hackers could be using alternate means of access to your networks such as dialing in to a modem, dialing into someone's PC, and from inside the organization. The NetRanger system from Cisco Systems Inc., the worldwide leader in networking for the Internet, is the industry's first enterprise-scale, real-time, network intrusion detection system (see Figure 20). It is designed to detect, report, and terminate unauthorized activity throughout a network. The NetRanger system can operate in both Internet and intranet environments to protect an organization's entire network.

The NetRanger system consists of two components: the Sensor and the Director. NetRanger Sensors, which are high-speed network appliances, analyze the content and context of individual packets to determine if traffic is authorized. If a network's data stream exhibits unauthorized or suspicious activity, such as a SATAN attack, a ping sweep, or the transmission of a secret research project code word, NetRanger Sensors can detect the policy violation in real

time. It would then forward alarms to a NetRanger Director management console and remove the offender from the network. The NetRanger Director is a high-performance software-based management system that centrally monitors the activity of multiple NetRanger Sensors located on local or remote network segments.

Figure 19   NetRanger system

Source: Cisco Systems

55

The NetRanger system incorporates proactive response functionality into the Sensor, allowing users to automatically eliminate specific connections identified with the unauthorized activity. The Director can remotely control the configuration of the Sensors, thereby allowing an organization to monitor the security of its connections from one centralized location. The Director can feed alarm information into an adjacent database archive to generate custom graphs and reports. The combination of the Sensor and Director provides for reducing costs and ensuring consistent security policy enforcement enterprise-wide.

The NetRanger system offers the following features:

◆ Real-time intrusion detection is transparent to legitimate traffic and network usage.

◆ Real-time response to unauthorized activity blocks offenders from accessing the network or terminates the offending sessions.

◆ A comprehensive attack signature list detects a wide range of attacks and can detect content and context-based attacks.

Locking Down Computers

Steel Security Cables

Software security systems can prevent hackers from getting access to your confidential data on your computer. In order to stop someone from physically taking your computer, you need to lock down your computer. Steel security cables provide an easy way to deter hardware theft. PC Security Kits from Computer Security Products Inc. protects any computer with standard security devices (see Figure 21). It comes with a hex fastener to protect internal components such as RAM from theft. The disc fasteners attach to your computer. A cable can be secured to an immovable object such as a table.

Figure 21. PC Security Kits

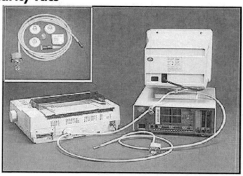

Source: Computer Security Products Inc.

Canterbury-Bankstown Library
http://cb.city/Library

Borrowed items 16/09/2018 14:30
20003520004

Item Title	Due Date
10007780113	8/10/2018
1. "Why "A" students work for "C"	
students and "B". s	
10006090335	8/10/2018
2. " International handbook of computer	
security / Jae	
10009333190	7/10/2018
3. Second chance : for your money, your	
life and our	
10005853810	7/10/2018
4 Wealth secrets of the 1% : the truth	
about money.	
10009567856	7/10/2018
5. The making of Donald Trump / David	
Cay Johnston	
10001016765	7/10/2018
6. Why the rich are getting richer : what	
is financia	

No of items: 6

* Indicates items borrowed today

To renew items contact 9789 9423
or online at http://cb.city/LibCat
After hours return facilities are available at
Campsie, Lakemba,Bankstown and
Chester Hill Libraries

Universal Drive Lock

Figure 22. Universal Drive Lock

Source: Innovative Security Products

In order to stop unauthorized users from physically inserting a floppy disk and transferring a virus, you have to secure the floppy drive attached to your computer. Universal Drive Lock from Innovative Security Products, provider of security devices for computers and office equipment, is a device that will lock up your external/ internal drives, including nearly all 3 1/2 in. and 5 1/4 in. floppy drives (see Figure 22). It can also lock up CD-ROM, Syquest, Iomega, tape back up, Macintosh floppy with flat bezels, and notebook/laptop drives. Universal Drive Lock offers the ability to leave a diskette or CD in the drive while using the lock.

Universal Drive Lock prevents the following:

◆ Introduction of an external virus to your computer and/or network

◆ Removal of sensitive files by unauthorized individuals

◆ Introduction of unauthorized software to PCs and networks

The Ultimate Security Kit

For companies that are looking for a complete security kit that will lock down a computer as well as notify others by sounding out an alarm, Innovative Security Products has a product called The

Ultimate Security Kit (see Figure 23). This kit will protect your PC or Macintosh computer with a 100+ decibel alarm if the unit is tampered with or if the cable is cut. Two steel lock down plates and a strong liquid adhesive offers up to 1000 lbs. of holding strength.

The Ultimate Security Kit prevents the following:

◆ Theft of the monitor

Figure 23. The Ultimate Security Kit

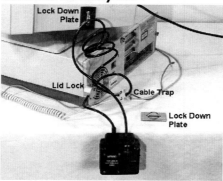

Source: Innovative Security Products

◆ Theft of internal components such as the CPU

◆ Theft of the keyboard or monitor

◆ Theft of the printer or other peripheral

Laptop Security

Computer theft is second only to auto theft. In 2005, there were 560,000 notebook computers stolen in the U.S. The losses in hardware, software, and data amounted to approximately $2 billion. Laptop security is critical, especially since laptops are becoming lighter and smaller. Thieves have a greater chance to conceal and abscond with your laptop within a few seconds. The data stored on a laptop, however, can be more valuable than the laptop itself, especially if you are a target of industrial espionage.

Here are some preventative measures that will help keep your laptop safe and secure:

◆ Keep good records. Serial numbers and a detailed description of your laptop will help the police trace it and will assist you if you need to make a claim with your insurance company.

◆ Use an etching tool to mark your name and phone number on your laptop.

◆ When staying in a hotel, never leave a laptop in the room unattended. If the hotel has a safe available, keep it there.

◆ Purchase separate insurance if you do not have business or home insurance that covers your laptop.

◆ Keep your laptop in an ambiguous carrying case. Use cases that look like a traditional briefcase or a piece of carry-on luggage.

Figure 24. Kensington Universal Notebook Security Cable Kit

Source: Computer Security Products Inc.

Another preventative measure is using a security cable. Master Lock, the maker of locking devices, and Kensington, the name in notebook security, have jointly developed the Universal Notebook Security Cable (see Figure 24). The security cable is a simple system for quick and easy installation. The lock fits into your computer's built-in security slot, a feature developed by Kensington and is now an industry standard.

To secure your portable computers, insert the lock into the built-in slot in your computer and wrap the cable around an immovable object like a table or desk. If no slot is available, the Security Slot Adapter Kit can be installed to secure the device. The simple and easy to install security cable provides the security for your laptop without having to carry bulky security equipment.

How to Deter Laptop Theft

With 69 percent of security risks reported from laptop theft, IT managers are always looking for ways to recover and deter laptop theft. Computer Security Products, Inc. in Nashua, NH has developed a product called the CompuTrace Theft Recovery Software to recover stolen laptops. CompuTrace uses the computer tracing technology and theft recovery system to silently and periodically call the CompuTrace Monitoring Center. It will work with any PC equipped with a modem. It is loaded onto the hard disk with a leading-edge stealth technology that hides inside from detection, even from anti-virus software. Once activated, CompuTrace will make regular calls to a toll-free tracking line, logging and archiving every call for analysis.

CompuTrace is scheduled to call its toll-free tracking line every five to seven days. It will detect when the modem is connected and not in use before calling. When it initiates a call, CompuTrace disables the modem speaker before making the regular call. With each call, the computer's serial number and originating telephone number are logged. If the laptop has been reported stolen, CompuTrace will use its theft recovery procedure to locate and recover the stolen computer. The Theft Recovery Team will coordinate the recovery of the stolen computer with local law enforcement to return your hardware and data.

CompuTrace is completely transparent from the operating system and applications. Since it does not appear in any directory, it is virtually impossible to remove. It cannot be erased off the hard disk by deleting files, formatting the hard disk, or even partitioning the hard disk.

CompuTrace benefits include:

◆ Reduces losses due to computer theft

◆ Can be incorporated into a theft deterrent program to reduce loses

◆ Easy to track and manage the company's computer assets

◆ Undetectable for maximum effectiveness

◆ Fully automated and maintenance free

◆ Compatible with all phone systems and popular security software products

Summary

Hardware security involves more than locking up the door to the computer room. Companies are using the Internet, Intranet, and Extranet to exchange information. Their employees use laptops wherever they go, carrying with them proprietary information. Hardware devices such as computer locks and smart cards help companies deal with these issues. Providing VPN access can reduce cost and keep data safe from intruders. Securing the organization's perimeter with alarms, surveillance cameras, and security guards make it transparent to intruders that security is enforced. Companies should consider all possible security breaches and implement a security solution that encompasses all security issues. With any security issue, the battle is always ongoing and requires newer tools and technologies to keep one step ahead of all intruders.

Chapter 4

Software Security

For many IT organizations, information security, such as access control and secure communications, are their primary objective to leveraging their businesses against their competitors.

The world is constantly changing and businesses are moving around a corporate network built on the Internet, Intranet, and Extranet. Vital information requires the fluidity of passage from both inside and outside the company's walls. In other words, appropriate security measures must be in place to safeguard the company's warehouse of information.

Security Breach

For businesses that have taken a stab at estimating the damage wrought by security breaches, losses per company averaged $203,606 in 2005, according to the most recent Computer Security Institute /FBI computer crime and security survey (of 639 respondents). (See Figure 4.1.)

The top three causes of losses in the study were viruses, unauthorized access, and theft of proprietary data. In a bit of good news, the study found that the fastest-growing category of breach – Website defacement – was responsible for the least amount of losses.

Figure 4.1: The Cost of Computer Crime

Losses by type of breach* (in $ millions)

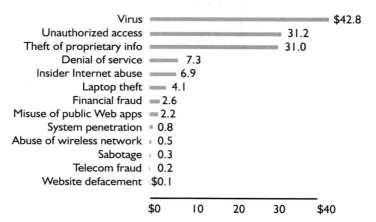

Virus	$42.8
Unauthorized access	31.2
Theft of proprietary info	31.0
Denial of service	7.3
Insider Internet abuse	6.9
Laptop theft	4.1
Financial fraud	2.6
Misuse of public Web apps	2.2
System penetration	0.8
Abuse of wireless network	0.5
Sabotage	0.3
Telecom fraud	0.2
Website defacement	$0.1

* 639 respondents reported a collective loss of $130 million.

Source: Computer Security Institute

Although three out of four organizations experienced a virus last year, nine out of every ten have a virus protection product in place, as shown in Table 1. With the increased growth in the Internet, Internet security is one of the major problems that companies have to deal with, but yet Table 1 shows that only six out of ten organizations have Internet/Intranet/Web Security products in place. As more organizations have a Web presence on the Internet and engage in e-commerce, we will eventually see an increase in the Internet security product used. Table 2 presents products and services organizations plan to purchase in the near future.

Table 1. Top 10 Information Security products and services now in use

Virus Protection	91%
Backup Storage	90%
Access Controls	85%
Physical Security	80%
Firewalls	74%
Client/Server Security	73%
LAN/WAN Security	67%
Disaster-Recovery Services	61%
E-mail Security	61%
Internet/Intranet/Web Security	60%

Source: Information Security

Table 2. Top 10 products and services organizations plan to buy in the "near future"

Encryption	32%
Training/Education	28%
Virtual Private Networks (VPN)	27%
Internet/Intranet/Web Security	27%
Firewalls	26%
E-mail Security	25%
Smart Cards	21%
Disaster Recovery Services	21%
Network/Communications Security	18%
Client/Server Security	18%

Source: Information Security

What is a Computer Virus?

A computer virus is a program that replicates and spreads by attaching itself to other programs. When the infected program is run, the virus executes an event. The event can be any of the following:

◆ Benign – displaying a message on a certain date

◆ Annoying – slowing performance or altering the screen display

◆ Catastrophic or damaging – damaging files, destroying data or crashing systems

For IT managers, they should address a virus as a subcategory of a malicious code. In general, a malicious code includes viruses as well as worms, Trojan horses, droppers, and bombs.

Worm

A worm is a program that replicates itself but does not infect other programs. It exists either on non-networked or networked computers. In a network setting, it copies itself to and from floppy disks or across network connections. In a non-networked computer, it can copy itself to various locations on your hard disks. In both cases, worms often steal and vandalize computer data.

Trojan horse

A Trojan horse is a program that is hidden inside a seemingly harmless program. When that program is run, the Trojan horse launches in order to perform a desired task, but also includes unexpected functions. Trojan horses do not replicate themselves. They can steal passwords, delete data, format hard drives, or cause other problems.

Dropper

A dropper is a program designed to avoid anti-virus detection, usually by encryption that prevents anti-virus software from noticing them. Typical functions of droppers include transport and installation of viruses. They wait on the system for a specific event, at which point they launch themselves and infect the system with the contained virus.

Bomb

A bomb is a malicious script or scheduling program that activates when a specific event occurs. Some bombs activate at a specific time, typically using the system clock. A bomb could be programmed to erase all DOC files from your hard disk on New Year's Eve or pop up a message on a famous person's birthday. A bomb might wait for the twentieth instance of a program launch and erase the program's template files.

Various Types of Viruses

Viruses can be thought of as special instances involving one or more of these malicious codes. They can be spread through droppers and use the worm idea to replicate themselves. They can act as Trojan horses by attaching themselves to an existing program, hiding inside the program, launching when the program launches, and committing unwanted acts.

The different types of viruses include:

1. Boot sector viruses or infectors residing in specific areas of the PC's hard disk, that are read and executed by the computer at boot time. Boot sector viruses can either infect the DOS boot sector or the master boot record. These viruses are loaded into memory during the boot process.

2. File infectors or parasitic viruses are viruses that attach themselves to executable files. These viruses wait in memory for the user to run another program. They replicate simply through the use of the computer.

3.   Macro viruses make use of programs such as Microsoft Office that ships with programming languages built-in. A macro virus is simply a macro for one of these programs, infecting such well-known programs as Microsoft Word. When a document or template containing the virus macro is opened in the target application, the virus runs and does its damage. They are also programmed to copy themselves into other documents to continually spread the virus.

4.   Multipartite viruses combine boot sector infection with file infection.

5.   Stealth viruses mislead anti-virus software that nothing is wrong. They retain information about the files they have infected, wait in memory, and intercept anti-virus programs that are looking for altered files. They give the anti-virus programs the old information rather than the new.

6.   Polymorphic viruses alter themselves when they replicate so that anti-virus software that looks for specific patterns will not find all instances of the viruses. Those viruses that survive can continue replicating.

7.   New and future viruses to come...

How Do Viruses Spread?

Viruses come from a variety of sources. About seventy-three percent of industry breaches come from viruses. Viruses, due to the way that they can attach themselves to legitimate software, can pass many security defenses. For example, the most common way to transmit a virus is through an infected floppy disk. In a study of major U.S. and Canadian computer users by Dataquest, the market research firm for the National Computer Security Association, the spread of viruses was shown to come from the following sources:

◆ Eighty-seven percent of users blamed an infected diskette.

◆ Forty-three percent of the diskettes responsible for introducing a virus into a corporate computing environment were brought from home.

◆ Seventy-one percent of infections occurred in a networked environment, making rapid spread of viruses a serious risk.

◆ Seven percent had acquired their virus while downloading software from an electronic bulletin board service (BBS).

◆ Six percent of infected diskettes included demo disks, diagnostic disks used by service technicians, and shrink-wrapped software disks.

As shown in the study, viruses also spread from networks such as the Internet. Viruses can be downloaded from trial programs, a macro from a specific program, or an attachment on an e-mail message. A virus that is delivered as an e-mail attachment, however, does nothing until you run it. By double-clicking on the attachment, you run this kind of virus. One way to protect yourself from this virus is simply never to open attachments that are executable files or data files for programs. Acceptably safe computing can be achieved by carefully crafted policies and procedures used in conjunction with antivirus and access control software.

What Are the Symptoms of Virus Infection?

Viruses remain free to spread into other programs because most common viruses give off no symptoms of their infection. Anti-virus tools are necessary to identify and eradicate these infections. Antivirus software designed to identify and remove known viruses is sometimes known as a vaccine. A vaccine works only for known viruses and may not be completely effective for variants of those viruses. Many viruses are flawed and do provide some tip-offs to their infection. Symantec, the maker of Norton AntiVirus software, offers some tips to watch for against viruses:

◆ Changes in the length of programs

◆ Changes in the file date or time stamp

◆ Longer program load times

◆ Slower system operation

◆ Reduced memory or disk space

◆ Bad sectors on your floppy

◆ Unusual error messages

◆ Unusual screen activity

◆ Failed program execution

◆ Failed system bootups when booting or accidentally booting from the A: drive

◆ Unexpected writes to a drive

Using Anti-Virus Software

Norton AntiVirus

Figure 2. Norton AntiVirus for Windows

To fully protect your corporate network from viruses, you will need to install some form of anti-virus software. Norton AntiVirus software from Symantec, as shown in Figure 2, is a good choice for Windows workstations and servers. The new features in version 5.0 let you quarantine infected files and automatically protect you against viruses as well as malicious ActiveX and Java applets. Norton AntiVirus runs in the background to keep your computer safe from viruses that might come from e-mail attachments, Internet downloads, floppy diskettes, software CDs, or a network.

Some key features included with Norton AntiVirus are:

◆ Quarantine – isolates infected files in a safe corner of your computer until you are able to repair them

◆ Scan and deliver – easily sends quarantined or other suspicious files to Symantec for evaluation and repair

◆ LiveUpdate – automatically retrieves new virus definitions from Symantec as often as once a week

◆ Protection against malicious codes – detects and removes dangerous forms of ActiveX code, Java applets, and Trojan horses

◆ 24 hour protection – runs constantly in the background to keep your computer safe from viruses

Dr. Solomon's Anti-Virus Deluxe

Figure 3. Dr. Solomon's Anti-Virus Deluxe for Windows

Another anti-virus software product that provides a defense against the spread of viruses is Dr. Solomon's Anti-Virus Deluxe from McAfee (see Figure 3). Dr. Solomon's WinGuard scanner and NetGuard provide 24-hour virus protection from Internet downloads, shared files, e-mail, floppies, and hard disks. It detects viruses in compressed and archived files. It also includes an SOS disk, which lets you boot from a clean diskette, even if your operating system will not load. With the SOS disk, it allows you to have a virus-free system before you install Dr. Solomon's Anti-Virus software. Dr. Solomon provides free automatic updates to the most current version of the software and protection updates to the hundreds of new viruses that appear each month.

Total Virus Defense

With over 22,000 existing viruses and over 300 new ones being created each month, protecting today's diverse networks from computer viruses is no easy task. The growth of distributed computing calls for a complete virus defense system that can fully protect all potential points of virus entry. Total Virus Defense 4.0 is a complete virus security solution from Network Associates, a provider of enterprise anti-virus solutions and Dr Solomon, a company in detection and cleaning technology. Total Virus Defense keeps your network protected at the desktop, the file and groupware servers, and the Internet gateways. It allows you to manage enterprise-wide virus security with its management tools and automated updating process.

Total Virus Defense ensures complete protection of your PC from all sources of viruses, including floppy disks, Internet downloads, e-mail attachments, networks, shared files, CD-ROM, online services, and even most popular compressed file types. Total Virus Defense is comprised of a suite of applications that protects all potential points of virus entry.

The Total Virus Defense suite includes:

◆ VirusScan - detects and removes viruses from desktop computers

◆ NetShield - detects virus infected files transmitted to and from the server in order to prevent the spread of viruses throughout the network

◆ GroupShield - scan groupware environments (Lotus Notes or Microsoft Exchange) to stop viruses before they are distributed to, or passed on by users

◆ WebShield - scans all inbound and outbound e-mail traffic passing through an SMTP e-mail gateway, automatically cleans or quarantines files, and sends alerts to system administrators

Total Virus Defense keeps your virus security solution current by providing tools to update all components of the product. Its AutoUpdate feature automatically updates desktop PCs and servers through scheduled downloads from a designated central server. Moreover, companies can automatically detect, remove, and create a cure for previously unknown viruses that could infiltrate corporate networks through AutoImmune. Through Anti-Virus Informant, it allows network administrators to proactively monitor virus defense capabilities. Finally, Total Virus Defense does not only detect and block viruses that are transmitted via Internet downloads, but it also scans e-mail attachments, stopping viruses before they have a chance to infect your system.

What is a firewall?

A firewall is a system or group of systems that enforces an access control policy between two networks. It is a security enforcement point that separates a trusted network from an untrusted one, such as the Internet (see Figure 4). It screens all connections between two networks, determining which traffic should be allowed and which should be disallowed. The security administrator determines in advance the security policy of how the firewall should set the rules to separate the two networks.

Figure 4. Firewall

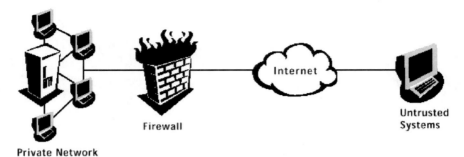

Private Network
Firewall
Internet
Untrusted
Systems

Source: McAfee

The most common firewall features include:

- ◆ Securing network access with a perimeter defense
- ◆ Controlling all connections into and out of the network
- ◆ Filtering data according to previously defined rules
- ◆ "Authenticating" users and applications to ensure that they are permitted to access internal resources
- ◆ Logging activities for security auditing purposes
- ◆ Actively notifying the appropriate people when suspicious events occur

Firewalls not only protect the internal corporate network from the public Internet, they are also being deployed internally. They can separate individual departments from the rest of the network. With internal firewalls, security administrators can apply different access control rules across a wide variety of working groups and network subnets. Internet firewalls enhance security by providing a layer of protection against internal breaches. For example, a firewall can protect the Human Resource department computing facilities to deter sensitive data from being accessed by other departments.

When you connect to the Internet, you are putting three things at risk:

- ◆ Your data – the information you keep on the computers
- ◆ Your resources – the computers themselves
- ◆ Your reputation – others using your identity

A firewall is the most effective way to connect a network to the Internet and still protect that network. The Internet presents marvelous opportunities for people to exchange ideas and information. At the same time, the risks are out there. Building a firewall requires significant expense and effort, and the restrictions it places on insiders can be a major annoyance. Once in place, firewalls offer significant benefits to protecting your systems and your data.

Some advantages of using firewalls are:

◆ Focusing your security decisions

◆ Enforcing security policy

◆ Logging Internet activity efficiently

◆ Limiting your exposure

Figure 5. Security Breaches

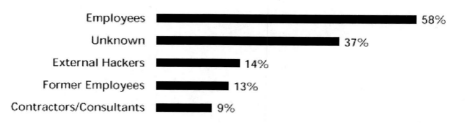

Source: Information Week/PriceWaterhouse Coopers, 2007

Firewalls offer excellent protection against network threats, but they are not a complete security solution. Certain threats are outside the control of the firewall and need to be addressed by other means. For example, a firewall works well in protecting your network from outsiders but it has no effect for someone behind the firewall. As shown in Figure 5, fifty-eight percent of security incidents originate from employees. The research surveys from Information Week/PriceWaterhouseCoopers indicate that more than half of all security breaches originate from employees, contractors, consultants, and other internal users.

Some of the weaknesses of firewalls are:

◆ Not protecting you against malicious insiders

◆ Not protecting you against connections that do not go through it

◆ Not protecting against completely new threats

◆ Not protecting against viruses

Packet Filter Firewalls

Firewalls serve as a security perimeter around a corporate network. For most organizations that want a high performance and easy to configure firewall, they will implement packet filter firewalls. In packet filtering, the firewall examines each incoming or outgoing IP packet header and checks its characteristics against a table of access control rules. As each individual packet enters the firewall, it looks at the header portion and compares the IP address and port of the source and destination against its rule base. If the address and port information are permitted, the packet proceeds through the firewall directly to its destination. If a packet fails this test, it is dropped at the firewall. Elaborate rules can be developed to allow or disallow certain packets into a company's private network.

Packet filtering works well in quickly filtering unwelcomed invaders. Packet filtering firewalls are fast because they operate at the network layer and make only cursory checks into the validity of a given connection (see Figure 6). Unfortunately, they have low security and no knowledge of application vulnerabilities. Once a connection has been approved by the firewall, the outside source is allowed to connect directly through to the target destination behind the firewall, potentially exposing the internal network to attack. For example, they allow a direct connection with untrusted external sources.

Figure 6. Packet Filter Firewall

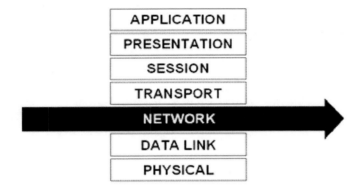

Source: Network Associates White Paper

Application Proxy Firewall

After the advent of the packet filter firewall, government agencies such as DARPA (Defense Advanced Research Projects Agency) and the U.S. Department of Defense started looking for a better approach to firewall security. Their research ultimately resulted in the application proxy firewall that offers very strong security. The application proxy firewall provides full application-level awareness of attempted connections by examining everything at the highest layer of the protocol stack (Figure 7). Because it has full visibility at the application layer, an application proxy firewall can easily see the granular details of each attempted connection up front and implement security policies accordingly .

Figure 7. Application Proxy Firewall

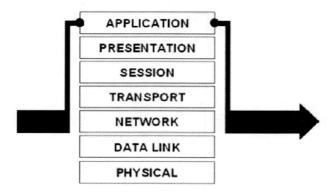

Source: McAfee White Paper, 2004

Application proxy firewalls also feature a built-in proxy function – terminating the client connection at the firewall and initiating a new connection to the internal protected network. Therefore, the firewall "proxies" connection never allows direct contact between trusted and untrusted systems. A proxy firewall makes it more difficult for hackers on the outside to exploit vulnerabilities on systems inside the firewall.

Proxy Server

Packet filtering alone is not enough to stop a break-in attempt because it does not prevent "spoofing" from outside the firewall. Spoofing is a way of using a valid internal IP address to pretend that the foreign system is inside your secure walls. As a result, many companies have migrated to proxy server firewalls. A proxy server resides between a client application such as a Web browser and a real server. A proxy server allows internal clients to access the Internet from behind a firewall. It intercepts all requests from clients within the firewall and forwards these requests to the real server. However, there is a downside to proxy servers. The overhead that is required to run an application proxy is considerably higher than that for a packet filter. Consequently, these companies experience significant slowness in network traffic.

Hybrid Firewalls

In 1998, a few vendors such as Check Point and Network Associates addressed this problem by designing what is called "hybrid firewalls." As the name suggests, hybrid firewalls combine the best of both worlds: the speed of a packet filter and the stringent security features of an application proxy. The way that hybrid firewalls work is by using packet filtering during peak hours when there is a lot of network traffic, but if the firewall perceives a threat, the application proxies take control. Furthermore, once a connection has been established through a proxy, all subsequent traffic is filtered, thereby balancing speed with security.

A Complete Firewall Security System

In recent years, companies are finding out that the Internet can serve as an indispensable technology. The Internet can link their company with customers, remote employees, suppliers, and business partners at a fraction of the cost. To remain competitive means that their private networks must be capable of extending out to the outside world. At the same time, this virtual corporation would require a security system such as a firewall to safeguard the vital information internal to the company.

With the increasingly sophisticated security threats from new technologies, having standalone firewalls to protect your network is not enough. An integrated network security that actively communicates with other security tools and responds to new attacks and modifies security measures accordingly is needed (see Figure 8). The role of the firewall has to evolve from a standalone system enforcing access rules into a distributed firewall system involving the integration of components throughout the network. A complete security system that is designed to keep out intruders must become seamlessly integrated with the firewall.

Figure 8. Distributed Firewall System

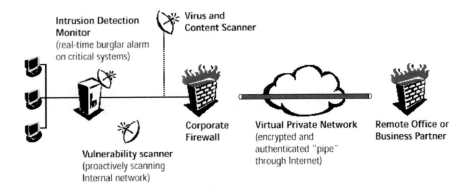

Source: MacAfee

A complete security system must encompass the following components:

♦ Firewalls that guard against unauthorized entry from outsiders or individual departments

♦ Vulnerability scanners that proactively scan the internal network for potential weaknesses or security holes

♦ Intrusion detection monitors that watch internal network traffic and servers for signs of attack

♦ Virus and content scanners that check for the presence of malicious code such as viruses, Trojan horses, or hostile Java and ActiveX applets

♦ A central event manager that provides meaningful integration between distributed security components (all monitors, sensors, and scanners)

Active Firewall System

To truly address the rapidly growing security threats, companies must not rely on passive firewalls that guard only the front entrance. Firewalls have to work in concert with other security components on the network to actively respond to changing threats. Network Associates, the supplier of enterprise network security and management software, has developed an active firewall system called the Gauntlet Active Firewall (see Figure 9). Gauntlet Active Firewall combines proactive vulnerability scanning, real-time intrusion detection monitoring, anti-virus scanning, and virtual private networking into a single active firewall system.

Figure 9. The Active Firewall

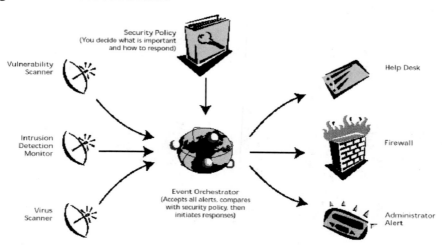

Source: McAfee

Gauntlet Active Firewall from Network Associates addresses the passive firewall problem by integrating multiple security products into a single system. The following scenario can demonstrate an example of how this system works. Every morning at 2:00am the vulnerability scanner is scheduled to run through a series of routine vulnerability scans. During one of these scans, it discovers that an employee has set her PC up as an insecure FTP server that exposes data on the private network to attack. The scanner forwards this information to the Event Orchestrator so that it can compare the customer's security policy to determine the appropriate course of action. After consulting the security policy, the Event Orchestrator instructs the firewall to shut down the FTP server until the IT staff arrives the following morning. The Event Orchestrator can also send a trouble ticket describing the problem to the help desk. When in the morning the user calls the help desk because her FTP service is not working, the IT staff, already aware of that, can then advise her of the security risks her actions have created.

What is Authentication?

Many people think of authentication in terms of passwords, but there are actually a variety of authentication mechanisms. These mechanisms can generally be categorized as one of the following:

◆ Something you are – field of biometrics, including techniques such as fingerprint scans, retina scans, voiceprint analysis, and so on

◆ Something you know – traditional password system

◆ Something you have – mechanisms such as challenge-response lists, one-time pads, smart cards, and so on

What is Encryption?

Encryption is the translation of data into a secret code. It uses algorithms to mathematically combine keys with the plain text to form encrypted or cipher text. It is the most effective security device because it requires you to have a specific key to unlock the data. It is a method of scrambling information so that only the intended receiver can use it. Any digital data can be encrypted, including e-mail messages, telephone calls, movies, pictures, and computer files. Today there are both hardware devices and software packages available for encrypting data.

There are two main types of encryption: *symmetric* (secret key) encryption and *asymmetric* (public key) encryption. Secret key encryption uses one key. Public key encryption uses a pair of keys called public/private keys.

Secret Key Cryptography

Figure 10. Symmetric Keys

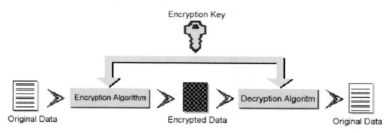

Source: Symantec Corporation

Before the creation of the public/private key method, a technology called symmetric (secret- key) cryptography was used. In this method, the secret key (a large binary number) is used to mathematically encrypt the communication, and the recipient uses the same key to decrypt it. It uses the same algorithm by having the encryptor and decryptor use the same key. In other words, two or more parties share a single key to encrypt and decrypt data. Secret key encryption is relatively fast and small. It is generated quite often in Web browsers each time they open a secure transaction. Using secret key cryptography, it is safe to send encrypted messages without fear of interception because the interceptor is unlikely to be able to decipher the message (see Figure 10). The problem with this method, however, is figuring out how to deliver the secret key to the recipient, either in another secure transmission channel or in person via a trusted courier.

Secret key cryptography provides confidentiality of information, but it falls short in two areas: key exchange and authenticity. In order to communicate securely using symmetric cryptography, all parties must have prior knowledge of the secret key. One way to transport the secret key is to hand-deliver the keys to potential communicators. If the secret key is intercepted, however, all communications are compromised. Moreover, this infrastructure is impractical when a large number of people need to communicate. If you have a large organization with people who need to exchange secret messages, you will need to have thousands (if not millions) of secret keys. In addition, secret key cryptography assumes that the parties who share a key rely upon each other not to disclose the key and protect it against modification. As such, it does not ensure authenticity of a sending party. For example, if Bob receives an encrypted message, he has no way of proving the identity of the sender.

The best known secret key system is the Data Encryption Standard (DES), published by the National Institute of Standards and Technology (NIST) as the Federal Information Processing Standards (FIPS) 46-2. NIST is an agency of the U.S. Department of Commerce's Technology Administration. The Federal Information Processing Standards Series of the NIST is the official series of publications relating to standards and guidelines mandated by the Secretary of Commerce. Since 1977,

NIST's DES has been the Federal Government's standard method for encrypting sensitive information. It is the most widely accepted, publicly available cryptographic system today. The algorithm standard has evolved from solely a U.S. Government algorithm into one that is used globally and adopted by the commercial sector.

Rivest, Shamir, and Adelman (RSA)

Rivest, Shamir, and Adelman (RSA) is the encryption technique that requires two keys, a public key that is available to anyone for encrypting messages and a private key that is known only to the recipient for decrypting messages. RSA is a potential encryption standard licensed to hardware and software vendors. Public-key encryption requires management of fewer keys for a given client-server environment than does private-key encryption. However, compared with DES, RSA entails more complex computations and therefore has a higher processing overhead. RSA requires two keys: the public key for encrypting messages is widely known, but the private key for decrypting messages is kept secret by the recipient.

Public Key Cryptography

A major advance in cryptography occurred with the invention of public key cryptography. As opposed to secret key cryptography, public key (asymmetric) cryptography uses a pair of keys that are mathematically tied together. The two keys consist of a "public" key and a "private" key. Using this "dual-key" method, a message can be encrypted with a public key, and the other (private) key used to decrypt the same message (see Figure 11). The public key may be distributed to the world because it is used only for encrypting a message. The private key must be kept confidential and be known only to its owner. The encrypted message can only be decrypted with its matching private key. This protocol is used with Secure Sockets Layers (SSL) technology, which is the standard protocol for secure, Web-based communications. Public key technology is a breakthrough because it solves the key management scalability problem associated with symmetric key encryption. It also reduces the possibility of key compromise during delivery.

Figure 11. Public/Private Keys

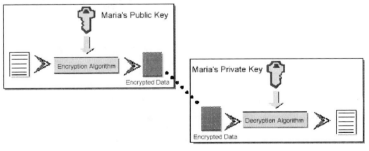

Source: Symantec Corporation

Prior to the invention of public key cryptography, it was virtually impossible to provide key management to large-scale networks. The number of keys required to secure communications among those users increased substantially as the number of users grew. For example, a network of 100 users would require almost 5000 keys if it only uses secret key cryptography. Doubling such a network to 200 users increases the number of keys to almost 20,000. The invention of public key cryptography resolved many problems with key management of large-scale networks.

Public key encryption, however, is bulky and slow. It does not easily encrypt a file once for a number of different people. If users lose their keys, they will not be able to decrypt those files encrypted with those keys. It also does not guarantee that John's public key is not someone else pretending to be John. As a result, most encryption systems use both types of encryption.

Both Types of Encryption

Public/private key pairs are very long and time consuming. To make the process fast and secure, both keys – symmetric key encryption and public key encryption – are used. In the scenario shown on Figure 12, Bill has a message that he wants to send to Maria. Bill uses a symmetric key to encrypt the document and then encrypt the symmetric key using Maria's public key.

Figure 12. Encrypt with symmetric and public keys

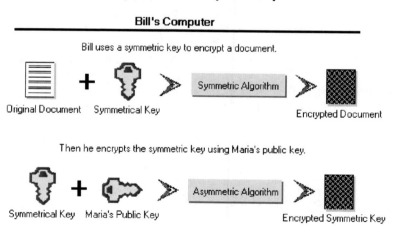

Source: Symantec Corporation

When Maria receives the encrypted message from Bill, she uses her private key to decrypt the symmetrical key (see Figure 13). Then Maria uses the symmetric key to decrypt the message.

Public/Private Key Technology in On-line Trading

Figure 13. Decrypt using private and symmetric keys

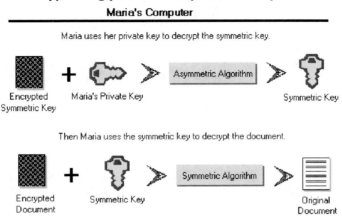

Source: Symantec Corporation

One of the major uses of public/private key technology is in the area of on-line trading. Security is a major concern for on-line investors as well as for on-line brokers. As rated by Gomez Advisors, an independent online financial service, the top five on-line brokers are E*Trade, DLJdirect, Discover Brokerage, Waterhouse, and Datek. In order to take precautions to ensure the security of customer's account information, these on-line brokers use encryption to safeguard against hackers intercepting a customer's user id and password and posing as the actual customer.

Figure 14. Public and Private Keys

Source: VeriSign Inc.

Figure 15. Encrypt and Decrypt

Source: VeriSign Inc.

To ensure security, on-line brokers use public/private key encryption technology to secure Web-based accounts of customers. As shown in Figure 14, the on-line brokerage firm keeps one key – the private key. It makes the other key – the public key – available to customers. As shown in Figure 15, anyone who finds the public

79

key can use it only to send the firm a private message. It cannot be used to decrypt messages sent to the firm or to imitate the firm. Therefore, the firm can send the public key to customers using e-mail or it can even post the key on its Web site.

In public/private key encryption technology, the customer's computer verifies the broker's server by checking the broker's digital signature and comparing it against the signature on record in a digital certificate. Digital certificates are sent by a third-party registrar such as VeriSign Inc. Then the customer's and broker's computers use a session key. As shown in Figure 16, the session key is used to encrypt all the data transferred during the session. The key ranges in length from 40 to 128 bits, depending on the level of security supported by the user's and broker's Web browser. This complicated conversion makes an intercepted message virtually impossible to decode. Even if a hacker happens to access a customer's account, funds can only be transferred to a customer's previously specified bank account.

Figure 16. Session key used to place an order	**Figure 17. Each transaction uses session key**

Source: VeriSign Inc.

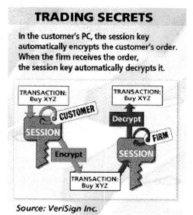

Source: VeriSign Inc.

As shown in Figure 17, each transaction uses a session key. For example, when a customer places an order, the transaction gets encrypted using the session key. When the firm receives the order, the firm uses its session key to decrypt the order. This process is not contiguous upon the next transaction. Therefore, when a customer buys another order, a new session key gets created. As such, this process ensures that no hacker can intercept and decode the transaction. Even if the hacker decodes this piece of transaction, the next one he/she gets will be entirely different.

What is Digital Signature?

Authentication generally has two components: one to prove that the information came from a specific user, and the second to prove that the information has not been altered. Authentication is possible through the use of a digital signature, a technique that uses public key encryption to "sign" electronic documents. A digital signature is a digital code that can be attached to an electronically transmitted message that uniquely identifies the sender. Like a written signature, the purpose of a digital signature is to guarantee that the individual sending the message really is who he or she claims to be. Digital signatures not only allow for strong authentication and data integrity, but also non-repudiation. Non-repudiation means that when participants transact business electronically, they cannot deny the transaction.

Digital signature schemes involve a two-step process:

1. Generating a message digest or hash of the message

2. Generating the signature by combining the message digest with the user's secret key

By adding the signature to the message, the integrity of the message is preserved. The digital signature confirms that the message has not been altered since you sign it because any changes to the message after you sign it will result in an invalid signature. All the trust in the signature, however, is tied to whether or not you can trust the signer's public key. If you cannot verify the public key belongs to the specific person, corporation, or authorized agent, then digital signatures can be forged.

What is a Public Key Infrastructure?

Since key management and digital signatures are based on public key technologies, good information security requires a Public Key Infrastructure (PKI). PKI is a system of digital certificates, Certificate Authorities, and other registration authorities that verify and authenticate the validity of each party involved in an Internet transaction. PKIs are currently evolving and there is no single PKI or even a single agreed-upon standard for setting up a PKI. Implementing public key encryption, digital signature, and other security services on a broad scale will require the establishment of many certificate authorities.

Entrust Technologies Inc., the global leader for solutions that bring trust to e-business, provides the Entrust/PKI to allow people to encrypt, digitally sign, and authenticate electronic transactions across all applications. Entrust/PKI works in a managed PKI. In a managed PKI, the users in one Certificate Authority (CA) can communicate securely with users from another, trusted, CA domain. A managed PKI provides a method for establishing and maintaining trustworthy electronic relationships between CAs. Entrust/PKI policy management provides security, flexibility, and ease of use through a wide range of PKI network policy options.

What is Kerberos?

Kerberos is an authentication system developed at the Massachusetts Institute of Technology (MIT). Kerberos was created as a solution to network security problems carried by insiders. It is designed to enable two parties to exchange private information across an insecure network connection. It works by assigning a unique key, called a ticket, to each user that logs on to the network. The ticket is then embedded in messages to identify the sender of the message. It provides the tools of authentication and strong cryptography over the network to help secure information systems across your enterprise.

What is Pretty Good Privacy?

Pretty Good Privacy (PGP) is a technique for encrypting messages developed by Philip Zimmerman. PGP is one of the most common ways to protect messages on the Internet because it is effective, easy to use, and free. PGP is based on the public-key method, which uses two keys. To encrypt a message using PGP, you need the PGP encryption package, which is available from a number of sources including the Massachusetts Institute of Technology.

PGP Enterprise Security Suite

PGP Enterprise Security Suite is a complete e-mail, file, disk, and network security from Network Associates. PGP users can send strongly encrypted files to non-PGP users with self-decrypting files. PGP Desktop Security, PGP Certificate Server, and PGP Policy Management Agent are applications for Win32, Macintosh, and UNIX environments. It integrates security and authentication for e-mail, files, and disks by integrating its various components:

- ◆ **PGP VPN Client** – utilizes either PGP or X.509 based certificates for secure VPN and remote Internet access to your network
- ◆ **PGP Desktop Security** – secure e-mail and files by encrypting and digitally signing for data protection and authentication
- ◆ **Certificate Server** – organizations can create and manage a unified public-key infrastructure that enables confidential communications across a corporate Intranet, Extranet, or the public Internet
- ◆ **Policy Management Agent** – enforces corporate security policies for e-mail communications across internal and external networks
- ◆ **PGP Software Developers Toolkit** – can incorporate trusted and peer-reviewed PGP cryptographic capabilities into new and existing applications

PGP Enterprise Security suite takes a pro-active role towards data security through quick and seamless integration of its tools. E-mails, files, and disks can be secured and authenticated as quickly as doing a "save file." It also supports current standards such as IPSec and X.509. X.509 is the most widely used standard for defining digital certificates. Although not officially approved, it is being implemented by various companies such as Microsoft and Netscape.

What is the Orange Book?

The real title, Trusted Computer System Evaluation Criteria, is a US government publication. It standardizes security system requirements and defines four broad categories of security for host-based environments:

◆ Minimal security (least)

◆ Discretionary protection

◆ Mandatory protection

◆ Verified protection (most)

The objective of the Orange Book is to:

1. Provide a way of assessing the level to which you can trust a given computer system.

2. Provide guidelines to manufacturers as to what to build into their system to satisfy various security needs.

3. Serve as a basis for specifying security requirements so you can purchase a coordinated security system.

In today's complex business environments, the Orange Book's security classifications are somewhat limited.

How to Enforce Security Policy across a Distributed Enterprise Network?

In the past, if IT managers planned to secure their companies' applications and systems, they had to use a variety of tools to gather all the reports. Axent Technologies Inc. has alleviated this process by creating a product called Enterprise Security Manager 5.0 (ESM). ESM allows administrators to check, manage, and enforce security policies from a central console. It lightens IT managers' workload by offloading the repetitive and redundant tasks associated with managing such a policy to computers rather than relying on human staff members.

ESM console and advanced reporting features provide a snapshot of security levels across the enterprise in a single graph. ESM is based on a manager / agent architecture. Software agents residing in servers and workstations gather pertinent data and send them to the ESM console. A single console can collect data from and manage up to 10,000 software agents.

Enterprise Security Manager offers the following features and benefits:

◆ **Consistency across platforms** – evaluates all systems based on a standard security policy

◆ **Broad platform support** – supports over 35 operating systems, including Windows NT, UNIX, NetWare, and OpenVMS

◆ **Dynamic configuration** – allows you to create customized policies to meet the needs of diverse environments

◆ **Integrated reporting capabilities** – allows you to go from enterprise-wide reporting to individual security settings with just a few clicks of the mouse

◆ **Intuitive Graphical User Interface (GUI)** – easy-to-use interface for configuring, managing and reporting on security policies across your enterprise

◆ **Corrects security problems fast** – corrects faulty security settings and updates groups of systems to security settings mandated in the security policy

◆ **Framework that works within your security environment** – integrates easily with existing security applications and processes, using Enterprise Security Manager Open Application Programming Interface

◆ **Manager/Agent architecture** – ESM's manager and agents can be different systems, allowing you to leverage your existing systems for managing and controlling security

◆ **Hierarchical approach** – scaleable to your enterprise network

Enterprise Security Manager provides an efficient means of managing, controlling and setting up your corporate policy. The manager/agent architecture relies on client/server technology. Only data that is absolutely necessary gets sent between managers and agents, resulting in less networking bandwidth used during security checks. All agents can be run manually or on a schedule, giving you flexibility to proactively manage your corporate computing environment.

Total Network Security

For all IT managers looking at a one-stop, network security solution, IBM is offering the industry's first e-business security solution. It enables companies to turn to a single vendor for all security software, hardware, and services needed when moving their businesses to the Internet. IBM's Integrated Security Solutions consist of three parts:

◆ IBM SecureWay FirstSecure - integrates security for Web-based systems with legacy-based systems

◆ Tivoli Availability - provides uninterrupted network services

◆ Tivoli Administration - provides centralized, consistent ways to manage a secure network

IBM plans to fulfill customers' needs by providing comprehensive solutions, ranging from encryption to virus protection, to simplify and allow their e-businesses to grow securely.

Internet Security Market

According to a study released in 2005 by the market research company International Data Corp. (IDC), in Framingham, Mass., the worldwide market for Internet security software grew from $2 billion in 1997 to an estimated $5.1 billion in 2004. Security threats continue to increase as more companies provide external access to their internal systems via the Internet for things such as Internet commerce, prompting many companies to increase spending on Internet security software. Based on the IDC study on a survey of 300 companies with more than $100 million in annual revenues, the market for Internet security software is expected to reach $5.1 billion worldwide in 2004 and grow to over $10 billion in 2006.

In general, the Internet software security market is expected to have a compound annual growth rate in terms of revenues of about 30 percent between now and 2006. IDC reports that the top three segments of this market between now and 2005 are:

◆ Firewall is the fastest growing segment with an estimated 40 percent compound annual growth

◆ Anti-virus software will be the largest segment of this market in 2006 and account for almost half ($6 billion) of the worldwide revenues from Internet security software

◆ Encryption software and software authorization, authentication, and administration

Security Protocols

SSL

With the growth of the Internet, many applications need to securely transmit data to remote applications and computers. SSL was designed to solve this problem in an open standard. Secure Sockets Layer (SSL) is the Internet security protocol for point-to-point connections. Many popular Web browsers such as Netscape Communicator and Internet Explorer use SSL to protect against eavesdropping, tampering, and forgery. In SSL, clients and servers make connections and authenticate each other. Once authenticated, a "secure pipe" is established across the Internet or Intranets and data can be securely exchanged (see Figure 18). SSL secures two applications by using strong encryption technologies from RSA Data Security, an encryption technology company.

Figure 18. Secure Socket Layer

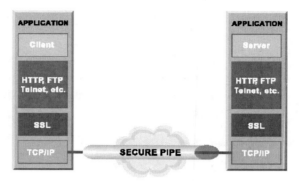

Source: RSA Data Security

Some practical applications of SSL are:

◆ client/server systems – securing database access

◆ financial – develop remote banking programs

◆ information systems – create remote access and administration applications

◆ travel industry – create online reservation systems and secure information transfer

IPSec

Internet Protocol Security (IPSec) is a set of protocols developed by the Internet Engineering Task Force (IETF) that provides encryption and authentication of TCP/IP traffic. It is the leading standard for cryptographically-based authentication, integrity, and privacy services. Authentication validates the communicating parties. Integrity makes sure the data has not been altered. Privacy ensures the data cannot be intercepted and viewed. At the IP layer, computers on a network communicate by routing datagram "packets." These datagrams contain data, destination addresses, source addresses, and other information. In a corporate local area network (LAN) or the Internet, these datagrams are transmitted "as is" and unencrypted. A malicious attacker can hijack, forge, or modify these packets. IPSec secures the network packets in order to create a secure network of computers over insecure channels such as the Internet. It enables users to communicate securely with a remote host over the Internet via Virtual Private Networks (VPNs). Where SSL authenticates and encrypts communications between clients and servers at the application layer, IPSec secures the underlying network layer to add security regardless of the application.

Some practical applications of IPSec are:

◆ Virtual Private Network (VPN) software and hardware - create secure networks over insecure means of transmissions such as the Internet

◆ Remote Access Software and Hardware - secure access to network resources

◆ Firewall Products - create secure VPN network tunneling to link business partners and members of the enterprise

S/MIME

Secure Multipurpose Internet Mail Extensions (S/MIME) is the electronic messaging standard that protects messages from unauthorized interception and forgery. S/MIME uses public-key encryption technology to secure transmission, storage, authentication, and forwarding of secret data. Where SSL secures a connection between a client and a server over an insecure network, S/MIME is used to secure users, applications, and computers.

Some practical applications of S/MIME are:

◆ Electronic Data Exchange (EDI) - digital signatures on contracts
◆ Financial Messaging - store and transfer bank statements
◆ Content Delivery - electronic bill payment
◆ Healthcare - create secure patient records and health claims

All three security protocols are based on the RSA algorithm for digital signatures and digital envelopes.

Table 3. Security Protocols Overview

Protocol	Summary
SSL (Secure Socket Layer)	Allows a "secure pipe" between any two applications for secure transfer of data and mutual authentication
IPSec (IP Security Protocol)	Standard for cryptographically-based authentication, integrity, and confidentiality services at the IP datagram layer
S/MIME (Secure MIME)	Guarantees the secure transmission, storage, authentication, and forwarding of secret data at the application level

Source: RSA Data Security

What is VPN?

Virtual Private Network (VPN) allows communications between sites using a public network such as the Internet to go over an encrypted channel. Since network communication over the Internet is vulnerable to "snooping" or electronic eavesdropping, setting up a VPN between two sites guarantees private communication between those sites. VPNs also represent cost savings over private networks such as leased line and frame relay because Internet access charges are based on local ISP. They reduce connectivity costs and deliver greater flexibility to network users.

A successful VPN deployment is much more than simple data encryption. A complete VPN solution includes:

◆ *Security* – granular access control, user authentication, standards-based data encryption to guarantee the security of network connections, authenticity of users, and privacy and integrity of data communications

◆ *Traffic Control* – bandwidth management, quality of service, and acceleration of data encryption/decryption to guarantee VPN reliability and performance

◆ *Enterprise Management* – comprehensive security policy that integrates enterprise-wide VPNs and centralized policy-based management

Remote Access Security Solution

The Internet has brought many corporations more flexibility in allowing their workers to telecommute or work in remote locations. At the same time, corporations need to ensure that remote users have access to the computer resources they need to do their job without sacrificing corporate network security. They have to prevent unauthorized users from gaining access to the corporate network by impersonating legitimate users. AXENT Technologies Inc., provider of information security, has a complete remote access security solution called Security Briefcase for Windows 95 and Windows NT. Security Briefcase integrates AXENT's Defender Security Server, PowerVPN and PCShield into a single solution managed from a central location (see Figure 19). Security Briefcase provides a complete enterprise policy-based solution by protecting the local disk, preventing unauthorized users from accessing corporate information, and securing the session over the Internet.

Figure 19. Security Briefcase

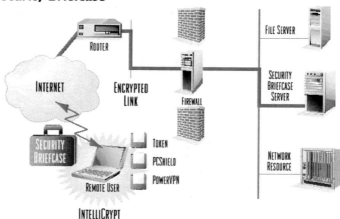

Source: AXENT Technologies Inc.

Defender

Passwords may be compromised with hacker tools such as password sniffers, network sniffers and dictionary attacks. Once passwords are stolen, unauthorized users can easily impersonate and access your files. Security Briefcase provides two-factor user authentication to secure remote and local access to sensitive resources and data. The two-factor authentication consists of something unique that the user has (a token) and something unique that the user knows (a PIN).

PowerVPN

Figure 20. Comparison between Firewall only and PowerVPN

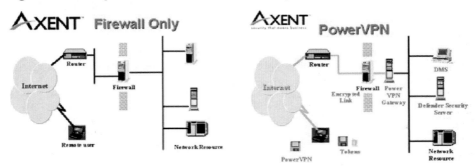

Source: AXENT Technologies Inc.

Sending data packets across public networks such as the Internet without encryption can cause your information to be compromised. Virtual Private Networks (VPNs) encapsulate data packets, securing your Internet communications. Therefore, unauthorized users cannot view, modify or intercept your data traveling over the unprotected network. PowerVPN does not require modification to the application software or the network. It can reduce your telecommunication costs by providing access directly to your private networks through any ISP, eliminating the need for costly toll-free numbers. Rather than dialing directly to the private network, users dial in to their local ISP and tunnel securely to the corporate network.

PowerVPN consists of a client that runs on a PC or laptop, and a gateway that is behind the firewall (see Figure 20). The secure and authenticated connection is between the PC that uses the PowerVPN encryption session and the PowerVPN Gateway at the corporate network. Unlike virtual private network from other firewall vendors, PowerVPN operates independent of the firewall, making firewalls instantly compatible with PowerVPN. PowerVPN works with all Winsock applications and does not require any modifications to applications. It increases throughput by compressing before encrypting the data.

PowerVPN's platforms and specifications are:

◆ **Encryption**: DES 40 (40 bits); DES (56 bits); Triple DES (2 Keys; 112 bits); Triple DES (3 Keys; 168 bits)

◆ **Clients**: Windows 3.x, 95, NT

◆ **Servers**: PowerVPN Gateway is available for Windows NT and Solaris

PCShield

Laptop computers are easily stolen or lost, but more importantly valuable corporate information resides on laptops. PCShield protects data on your PC from unauthorized users by providing automatic file encryption, decryption and centralized key management all in one product. PCShield provides centralized administration of PC and laptop security, protecting data on PCs, laptops, file servers, and the network. A central database contains all user accounts, groups, file access control rules and audit standards, making it possible to know which computers each user can access. This entire secure authentication is integrated into the product, making the process transparent to the Windows operating systems and applications.

PCShield automatically protects newly created files from unauthorized access. It secures files that are stored locally, on file servers, on floppy drives, or even files transmitted across the network. PCShield adds an access control label to each protected file so that the protection stays with the file wherever it resides. PCShield automatically encrypts data without having the user even "push a button" to make sure the information is protected. When a PC is left unattended or connected to the network, it requires users to re-enter their password to regain access to the system. Information cannot be accessed on a protected stolen laptop. Even if someone in your office tries to get to your "personal" information while you are away from the office, they will be denied access.

Like the PowerVPN product, PCShield has various encryption methods:

1. Data Encryption Standard (DES)
2. Triple DES
3. The exportable AXENT encryption method

Doing Business over the Internet

Certificate Authorities

Business is built on trust. On the Internet, that trust may be compromised without having some form of security. In order to secure your data over the Internet, certificate of authorities (CA) are the only way to go. They involve complex software that generates and manages digital certificates. CA can be built either in-house or outsourced to a third party. Companies who plan to go either route must weigh the cost versus benefit within their budget and then decide on which one makes more sense.

Some issues of concern for building an in-house CA server include:

◆ Having a good working knowledge of public key cryptography

◆ Deciding on either top-down CA or cross-certification

◆ Looking into performance and scalability

◆ Making sure their CA software uses a standard certificate to ensure that different packages can communicate

◆ Having CAs comply with LDAP (lightweight directory access protocol) to make it easier to store certificates

◆ Deciding on price and protection

◆ Deciding on whether having control of your own security is an issue

Some issues of concern for outsourcing to a third-party CA include:

◆ Deciding on what it takes to support certificates with people and budget

◆ Speed of deployment

◆ Leveraging the third-party's expertise and high security facilities

◆ Determining if burden of handling CA should be placed on a third-party

◆ Deciding on whether having control of your own security is an issue

◆ Trust in the third party as well as in its policies and practices

Whether it is developed in-house or supplied by a third party, a CA has a straightforward task: it verifies the identity of end-users. It accomplishes this task by issuing certificates — unique, encrypted digital IDs — that are attached to e-mail, transaction records, or files sent over the Internet or corporate intranet. A certificate is like a digital passport that lets the recipient know that the sender is who he or she claims to be.

All CAs are based on public key cryptography and typically have three components:

◆ A database that stores public keys

◆ A cryptographic engine that generates the actual certificate

◆ A PKI (public key infrastructure) engine that tracks the expiration date of issued certificates

E-mail Security

E-mail has become such an integral part of the working world that it also poses a number of significant security threats. For example, e-mail provides a direct link to users or groups of users. The accessibility given by the Internet provides hackers with a direct line to personal and corporate in-boxes. Viruses and malicious active content, such as rogue Java applets, can be attached to incoming messages. A simple mouse click by the targeted user is all it takes to activate them. They can damage or steal data or crash a machine. Spam, or junk e-mail, can flood in-boxes with time-wasting, unnecessary or inappropriate content. Spam attacks can clog LANs with illegitimate traffic or strain the Internet gateway.

Yet many companies and individuals do not give much thought to e-mail security. Unlike other security initiatives, e-mail requires a more ongoing challenge than installing a firewall. One tool that can be used in desktop and in corporate settings is virus-scanning software to scan for e-mail viruses. But there is not a single methodology that can protect a user or company from all e-mail based threats. Hackers can exploit a variety of district weaknesses surrounding e-mail.

E-mail poses a number of security holes. Among the most prominent are:

Table 4   Security holes

Vulnerability	Problem it poses	Possible solutions
Unencrypted e-mail	Can be read by unknown and unauthorized third parties while it traverses the Internet, or even by unauthorized employees within the intranet	E-mail encryption, virtual private networking solutions
Malicious attachments and viruses	Unsuspecting users may open e-mail attachments from unfamiliar senders and unleash viruses or malicious active content onto their desktops	Virus scanning products for both the client and the firewall
Spam	More of a nuisance than a security problem, spam (junk e-mail) can clutter the LAN and in-boxes with unwanted and often inappropriate messages	E-mail filters

Regardless of policies and products, e-mail security will remain a moving target as hackers continue to find their way around existing barriers and safeguards. Some suggestions that users can use to secure their e-mail include:

◆ Not opening attachments from unfamiliar sources

◆ Reporting instances of spam

◆ Using encryption when sending highly sensitive information across the Internet

Spam

Spam is an unwanted e-mail. In a Monty Python television skit, a group of Vikings in a restaurant sing about the meat product, "Spam, spam, spam, spam, spam, spam, spam, spam, lovely spam! Wonderful spam!" until told to shut up. As a result, something that keeps being repeated to great annoyance was called spam, and computer programmers picked up on it.

Note: Tips to avoid getting spam

1. *Protect your e-mail address.* Spammers either buy lists of e-mail addresses or use software programs that mine the addresses from the Internet. If your address is posted in discussion groups, on Web sites, chat rooms, etc., chances are it will end up on one or more of these lists. Only post your address publicly when absolutely necessary.

2. *Set up multiple e-mail accounts.* If you do participate regularly in online activities where you post your address, set up another e-mail account. Reveal it only to close friends and family.

3. *Use spam filters.* Many e-mail programs, such as Outlook Express, have built-in tools that block messages sent from certain addresses or that filter messages based on key words you define. Check the online help files for your e-mail software.

4. *Use anti-spam software.* You can install software designed to eliminate spam. Some work by matching incoming messages against a list of known spammers; others block messages that don't match an approved list of acceptable addresses. Check out the latest anti-spam programs at Download.com.

5. *Report violators.* A number of government agencies and private groups accept complaints. Whether they can do anything to stop the deluge is an unanswered question. Forward spam to the Federal Trade Commission at uce@ftc.gov.

Access Control

Access Control refers to mechanisms and policies that restrict access to computer resources. Security software should address the following security needs:

◆ Public/private key on-the-fly encryption/decryption
◆ Centralized management
◆ Mobile and remote users
◆ Access control for multiple users at a single machine

ACL, short for *access control list*, a set of data that informs a computer's operating system with which permissions, or access rights, that each user or group has to a specific system object, such as a directory or file. Each object has a unique security attribute that identifies which users have access to it, and the ACL is a list of each object and user access privileges such as read, write or execute.

Anywhere Access via the Internet

Corporations have discovered the tremendous benefits of the Internet to provide remote access for employees, partners, suppliers, and customers. In order to connect these users to their private networks, most companies still use costly, private dial-up to connect remote users. In addition, companies must install and configure necessary encryption and tunneling software for a large number of mobile users. Sun Microsystems i-Planet product is designed to leverage the cost of computing and offer access to your corporate intranet from the Internet. Sun intends to lower the total cost of ownership for remote access and increase enterprise productivity.

As a remote access solution, i-Planet software uses Java to eliminate the need for remote users to dial into a corporate modem pool or use security and authentication software tied to a laptop. By using the Internet standard for remote access, i-Planet software enables remote users to access the private network from various technologies such as cable modems, DSL or ISDN (see Figure 21). With i-Planet, users can use any browser enabled with Java technology to read e-mail, download data, check their appointment calendar, and access other enterprise information.

Figure 21. i-Planet Topology

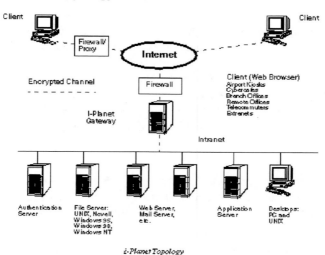

i-Planet Topology

Source: Sun Microsystems

The i-Planet architecture is a server software-based solution that does not require any client installation, management, or configuration. With i-Planet software, users only need a Web browser and an Internet connection. The client application is either pushed to the client as HTML Web pages or a Java applet that is downloaded on demand. Once users clear the authentication, i-Planet creates a virtual private network on the fly. User authentication is handled over an encrypted Secure Sockets Layer (SSL) channel between the client Web browser and i-Planet authentication subsystem.

i-Planet software provides secure remote access for authorized users for the following clients:

- ◆ **Internal HTML front ends and Web sites** – provides secure access to intranet applications and Web pages
- ◆ **E-mail access** – provides access to IMAP-compatible mail servers
- ◆ **Calendar access** – supports the Common Desktop Environment (CDE) calendar and Sun Calendar Server applications
- ◆ **X11 and PC applications** – enables you to run existing mission-critical PC or X11 applications without any change to the applications
- ◆ **File access** – optimizes mailing large files and attachments by delegating as many tasks to be performed on the server as possible to improve performance for remote clients
- ◆ **Terminal emulation** - enables the use of a local telnet client and VT100 emulator to allow encrypted telnet sessions from the Internet

The minimum requirements to run i-Planet are:

Client Systems

Supported Web browser (Client):

- ◆ Netscape Communicator v4.04 or Internet Explorer v4.0 with:
  - ➢ SSL v3.0
  - ➢ JavaScript software
  - ➢ JDK 1.1 software

Server Systems

- ◆ Solaris 7 or Solaris 2.6 operating environment on the SPARC platform
- ◆ Two servers are recommended:
  - ➢ Gateway
  - ➢ Platform and Application
- ◆ 300 Mbytes of disk space
- ◆ 64 Mbytes of memory

Summary

In this day and age, computer security has to do with protecting your sensitive information from outsiders, as well as insiders. Companies looking to protect their organization need to consider a security policy that covers all aspects of computer security. In terms of software security, financial losses occur not just from hackers going through the Internet and into your private network, they can also occur from within the organization. Security tools such as firewalls, anti-virus software, and encryption will help companies deter access to unauthorized users. Believing that your environment is secured is not enough; you have to take a proactive approach to maintaining security and making sure that newer technologies are being implemented to stop the sophisticated hacker tools available to everyone. Providing a safe and secure environment will protect your investments for the coming years.

Chapter 5
Personnel Security

Every staff position that interacts with the computer system should be evaluated from a security perspective. Establish criteria for filling each position; spell out the process to be used to evaluate candidates, screen applicants, and conduct background checks. Specify the training program for new employees.

Define each position clearly, describing its functions. Assess the sensitivity level. Sensitivity level is determined by the degree of harm a person could cause in that position: For instance, a person might be in a position to steal or disclose confidential data, interrupt critical processing functions, commit fraud, or steal resources. What type of computer access will be needed for the position? Employees should be given only the access needed to perform their duties.

Segregation of duties is an important control to ensure that employees do not perform incompatible duties. This means you must allocate responsibilities so that a single employee cannot perpetrate an error and cover it up in the normal course of his or her duties. You'll need checks and balances to prevent or catch irregularities, so that the duties of one person automatically check the work of another.

Functions such as systems analysis, programming, computer operations, and data control should be segregated. The electronic data processing (EDP) department should be organizationally independent of the operating departments. It should not have the authority to correct data entered by users in other departments.

Screening

Before you hire anyone for a sensitive position, perform a pre-employment background check. (For less sensitive positions, post-employment screening may be sufficient.) For highly sensitive positions, the background check should provide positive evidence that the candidate can honestly perform the duties required.

The applicant's prospective supervisor should not conduct the background check; the personnel department or an independent agency should do it.

A significant percentage of applicants lie either on resumes or in interviews. These individuals should be rejected not only because they may not be qualified but also because they lack the integrity required for sensitive positions.

Many individuals will not divulge a criminal past to prospective employers. If the employee thereafter commits a criminal act that affects others, the employer may be held liable. Employers have a legal obligation to thoroughly investigate their employees' backgrounds—without violating an employee's privacy. Check an applicant's previous address, professional and bank references, credit history, criminal record, and previous employers.

When applicants lie about their work history, they tend to:

◆ Increase the amount of time they have spent at a job
◆ Create fictitious employers
◆ Boost their salary levels
◆ Tell you that their employer has gone out of business
◆ Exaggerate job duties and inflate job titles
◆ Falsely claim to be self-employed or independent consultants

Candidates may also fabricate educational credentials and professional experience. Having only a year or two of college, they may claim that they have a degree. A person may have even assumed the identity or bought their degrees from unaccredited mail-order universities. Some fabricate honors and awards. Others may list fake publications on their resumes. Applicants should be asked to provide copies of their publications and proofs of honors and awards.

Many employers do a poor job of checking references. They either don't bother with the references or ask superficial questions. To avoid legal hassles, all applicants should be required to sign a release form. The applicants should promise to hold their references harmless for what they say. Before any formal offer is made, if the reference check is not acceptable, it's not necessary to give the candidate a specific reason for not being chosen. Keep records of reference checks to refute allegations of discriminatory or illegal actions. A conscientious reference check may also defend your company in any later litigation over the employee's actions.

You can access hundreds of public sources to check an applicant's background. Checking from public sources does not require the applicant's permission. Public records often contain conviction records and in some jurisdictions, arrest records.

Federal agencies collect a vast amount of data on individuals. The FBI's Identification Division contains the largest repository of criminal records in the United States. The Freedom of Information Act (FIA) allows you to access many government files, including criminal conviction records. A conviction in itself is generally not a sufficient reason to deny the applicant the job; the conviction should relate to the job you're trying to fill.

The financial and credit records of prospective applicants can be accessed through credit bureaus and private investigative agencies. The Fair Credit Reporting Act governs investigative consumer reports, which are frequently used by prospective employers to screen candidates.

Corporate records and limited partnerships records are public. These records are one way to tell if the applicant actually owned a business, and for how long.

From court records, you can learn if the applicant was a participant in any civil or criminal litigation. City and county filings may give you information about such financial factors as whether there are any liens against the applicant. Additional sources of financial information are real property records and tax rolls. Financial situations may have an effect on a person's ability to perform the job; a financially troubled candidate may have a greater incentive to commit fraud.

The following companies perform pre-employment background verification:

◆ Accurate Data Services: http://www.acudata.com

◆ American Background: http://www.americanbackground.com/

◆ American Labor Resources: http://www.amlabor.com/

◆ Background Check International, LLC: http://www.bcint.com/

◆ Barrientos & Associates: http://www.emcsat.com/

◆ EMPFacts Factual Data: http://www.employmentscreen.com/

◆ Indepth Profiles: http://www.idprofiles.com/

◆ Informus Corp.: http://www.informus.com/

◆ Justifacts: http://www.justifacts.com/

◆ On-Line Screening Services, Inc.: http://www.onlinescreening.com/

◆ Pennell & Associates: http://www.pennellinvestigations.com/

◆ PEV: http://pev.frickco.com/

Legal Agreements

Insist that new hires in sensitive jobs sign employment agreements with non-disclosure provisions. The agreement should specify:

◆ Scope of the employee's duties

◆ That the employee will work solely for your organization and may not work anywhere else without advance written permission

◆ That the organization is entitled to reap the benefit of the employee's work product

◆ That the employee will not reveal secrets to unauthorized individuals, within as well as outside the organization

◆ The conditions for terminating the employee

◆ That the employee will return all materials, including notes, handbooks, computer programs, commercial documents, and software at your request, and always at the end of the employment term

◆ That the employee may not keep any copies of items owned by the organization

◆ The limitations on the types of work the employee may do after leaving the organization

◆ That the employee will not engage in any unfair business practices, including corporate spying or engaging in a business that competes with the employer's business

◆ That the employee will abstain from any activity that may hurt the employer or its interests

Training New Employees

Training new employees in computer security responsibilities and duties is a highly effective way of enhancing security. You may want to limit a new employee's access to the computer system until security training is completed, but it's also essential that computer security training be ongoing.

These are some of the issues to be addressed during training:

◆ The organization's data back-up policies

◆ The type of data that should be encrypted

◆ How the data encryption keys are managed

◆ What types of data may be shared with colleagues

◆ What types of data are available to the public

Performance Appraisal

Performance and skill level of employees should be routinely documented, using formal performance evaluation systems. Give employees feedback about their performance regularly.

An effective review procedure can help prevent job frustration and stress. It can also help maintain employee morale. It's important to be concerned about the threat of psychological dissatisfaction. Disgruntled employees may do intentional damage. Moreover, job turnover associated with dissatisfied employees disrupts the operations and maintenance of computer systems. Discontent can act as a catalyst for computer crime or sabotage. Watch for possible indicators of discontent, such as:

◆ Low quality or low production output

◆ Complaints

◆ Late arrivals

◆ Excessive absenteeism

◆ Putting off vacations

◆ Excessive unwarranted overtime

Quick action, like communicating with the employee on one-to-one basis, can significantly minimize job discontent.

Exit Procedures

Special security issues arise when an employee leaves. An employee may leave on mutually agreeable terms, including retirement, promotion, accepting a better position at another company, or transferring willingly to another department. An employee may also leave on unfriendly terms, as when the employee is fired, unwillingly transferred to another department, forced into retirement, or demoted.

For a mutually agreeable termination, follow a standard exit procedure. Upon leaving the organization, employees should be required to return badges, keys, and company materials. Change their access codes and passwords, and even locks if necessary.

Data files, especially encrypted files and the keys to decrypt them, other documents, and all backed-up files should be returned. Don't let the employee keep copies of anything; you should both sign an agreement attesting that all copies have been returned.

Employees can cause considerable damage if terminated, for example, they may:

◆ Intentionally input erroneous data

◆ Erase data files and destroy back-ups

◆ Make copies of data files for personal use or for competitors

◆ Create "random" errors that are difficult to trace and costly to correct

While most employees can do some harm to the computer system, systems personnel can do the most. From a security perspective, termination of systems personnel requires great caution. For example, systems personnel may delete or destroy data or program files. They may also place logic bombs to harm the system (erase data, deny access, etc.), activating the code after their departure. They can set these in place long before they're even notified of termination. Protect your organization with controls over modification of system files.

When an employee is leaving on unfriendly terms, his or her access to the computer system should be restricted as quickly as possible. These accounts should be closed before or at the same time the employee is notified of the termination.

Chapter 6

Network Security

Networks may be broadly classified as either wide area networks (WANs) or local area networks (LANs). Network security is needed for both LANs and WANs. The computers in a WAN may be anywhere from several miles to thousands of miles apart. In contrast, the computers in a LAN are usually closer together, such as in a building or a plant. Data switching equipment might be used in LANs, but not as frequently as it is in WANs.

On the Internet, security is needed to prevent unauthorized changes to one's web site. For businesses selling information-related products over the Internet, such as software vendors that may allow their paying customers to download upgrades, there has to be a way to discriminate between paying customers and non-paying individuals. Online access controls, such as passwords, ID numbers, access logs, and device authorization tables, prevent improper use or manipulation of data files and programs. They insure that only those persons with a bona fide purpose and authorization have access to data processing. Many systems use tests that are maintained through an internal access control matrix that consists of authorized user code numbers, passwords, lists of all files and programs, and a record of the type of access each user is entitled to have to each file and program.

Security administrators face the risk that an attacker will be able to break into the organization's network. The attacker may be anyone with motivation to obtain access. The attacks may range from direct attacks by both hackers and insiders to automated attacks such as those using network worms. Such an attacker might obtain:

Read access: The attacker is able to read or copy confidential information.

Write access: The attacker is able to write to your network. This includes the ability to infect the system with a virus or plant Trojan horses or back-doors. The attacker may also destroy confidential information by deleting it or writing over it.

Denial of service: The purpose of some attacks is simply to deny authorized users of normal network services. An attack may be launched which consumes CPU time, network bandwidth, or fills up memory.

Security risks in using a server on the Internet include inappropriate configuration of FTP (file transfer protocol) settings. If FTP access is allowed to your server, it is essential to properly configure it to prevent unauthorized modifications to files.

There must be a secure communication link of data transmission between interconnected host computer systems of the network. A major form of communication security on the network is cryptography to safeguard transmitted data confidentiality. Cryptographic algorithms may be either symmetric (private key) or asymmetric (public key). The two popular encryption methods are link-level security and end-to-end security. The former safeguards traffic independently on every communication link, while the latter safeguards messages from the source to the ultimate destination. Link-level enciphers the communications line at the bit level; data is deciphered upon entering the nodes. End-to-end enciphers information at the entry point to the network and deciphers information at the exit point. Unlike link-level, security exists over information inside the nodes.

There should be a general or a specific list of authorized users. Questions to be answered are:

Who is allowed into the facilities?

When may they enter?

What is the purpose of the visit?

A variety of tools are available to help the security manager implement the security plan. These include:

Encryption tools

Route and packet filtering

Firewalls

Each company should have a network security policy. Each company should also have an internal corporate security policy. An organization must decide how critical it is to protect the integrity of its computing system and how critical is the security of its web site.

The internal security plan should be distributed to everyone who uses the facilities. Employees should be given written guidance upon the proper use of passwords. They should be informed about the types of words that should not be used as passwords. There should be a policy concerning how frequently the password is to be changed.

There must be positive authentication before a user can have access to the on-line application, network environment, nature of applications, terminal identification, and so on. Information should be provided on "a need to know" basis only.

Access controls should exist to use a specific terminal or application. Date and time constraints along with file usage may be enumerated. Unauthorized use may deactivate or lock a terminal. Diskless workstations may result in a safer network environment.

Passwords

Most local area network or communication software packages contain encryption and security features. Passwords are included in virtually every package. However, passwords often do not provide adequate protection. People generally don't select good passwords or change them frequently enough. From a security perspective, it is often not too difficult for hackers to breach security by guessing passwords.

Each company should have a password policy. Many hackers are able to guess passwords because people tend to make certain mistakes. Passwords should never be shared with other individuals. Passwords should not be written down. Passwords should be easy to remember. If one needs to write down the password to remember it, the purpose of the password is defeated. Users should be given certain guidelines:

◆ Users should not select a password that is a word in English or any language. Hackers often use dictionaries to guess passwords. Passwords should not consist of words or names found in encyclopedias.

◆ Users should avoid patterns like *123456, 12468, asdf* or *qwerty*, from the keyboard.

◆ Geographical names, such as Vegas or Florida, should not be used.

◆ Many computer systems require the password contain numerals in addition to alphabetic characters. Many people then use a word, appended by a single number, usually one (e.g., CAT1 or 1CAT). Hackers are easily able to overcome this. They know that most people will select a word and append it with the numeral one.

◆ Users should be encouraged to use a combination of upper and lower case characters. Non-alphabetic characters can also make it more difficult for hackers to guess passwords.

◆ An excellent technique to create a password is to use the first letter of a phrase to create a password. For example, the phrase, "*I Was Born In New York*" would yield the password "*IWBINY*." This is not a word that is easily guessed. It is also easy for the user to remember.

◆ Users should be required to change their passwords at periodic intervals. This can be accomplished by programming the computer system to require the users to provide new passwords. The system should check to ensure that users do not use the same password again, or select a password that they have used over the last few months. A history should be kept of older passwords to prevent the users from using the same passwords again.

◆ All users should be provided with security guidelines. It is very beneficial to give new users a small course in taking security precautions and selecting a good password.

Users must be motivated and they must understand why selecting a good password is essential. The following web site provides users with information about selecting a good password. It also helps users evaluate the strength of their existing password(s). *http://www.symantec.com/*

Passwords provide good protection from casual or amateur hackers. Professional or experienced hackers are typically able to bypass the password system. The UNIX environment is quite common and is frequently used. Software programs are available that can assist new hackers, even those with limited knowledge, to find or guess passwords. The aim of most hackers is to obtain unlimited access to the computer system. This is typically accomplished by:

◆ finding bugs or errors in the system software

◆ taking advantage of an incorrect installation

◆ looking for human errors

Many hackers are authorized users, with limited access to the system, trying to get unlimited access. These hackers will have a valid user id and password, and will look for weaknesses in the system that may be exploited.

In most UNIX systems, passwords are stored in an encrypted file. Some systems use a shadow password file where the original data is stored. Passwords are generally encrypted using the Data Encryption Standard (DES) algorithm. A key is used to encrypt and decrypt passwords.

The type of encryption method used is essentially irreversible. While it is easy to encrypt a password, it is extremely difficult, almost impossible, to decrypt it. It is nonetheless possible for hackers to discover the passwords through brute force. If a password consists of only six lowercase characters, a hacker can find the password rather quickly. It is, therefore, critical that passwords for accounts that are likely to attract hackers not consist of simply lowercase characters.

A serious design flaw can sometimes result in the creation of a "universal password." Such a password satisfies the requirements of the login program without the hacker actually knowing the true and correct password. In one case, for example, a hacker could enter an overly long password. The overly long password would end up overwriting the actual password, thus allowing the hacker unauthorized access.

Modem Connections

Any time a user is able to connect to the network using a modem, additional risks are introduced into the system. Certain precautions can be taken to minimize risks associated with dial-in modems.

It is important to realize that simply keeping the telephone number secret is not sufficient. Many hackers dial the entire prefix of telephone numbers and they could randomly discover your telephone number.

In the past, many companies used dial-back techniques to reduce the dial-in modem risk. Nowadays, with caller-id, the same objective may be accomplished. Essentially, the network will allow users access only from certain pre-identified telephone numbers. The obvious disadvantage of this technique is that the telephone numbers of authorized users must be arranged in advance. This makes it especially difficult for users who travel.

Another way to minimize risk of dial-in modems is to use hardware encryption devices on both ends of the connection. These devices, however, tend to be expensive.

A good telecommunications software program will have numerous protocol options, enabling communications with different types of equipment. Some communications programs do error checking of information or software programs received. Desirable features in telecommunications programs include menus providing help, telephone directory storage, and automatic log-on and redial.

Saboteur's Tools

While in recent years ingenious procedures have been developed to preserve computer security, many computer systems are still astonishingly insecure. Saboteurs may use a wide variety of tools and techniques to overcome security. Some of the methods are as follows:

Trojan Horse: The saboteur places a hidden program within the normal programs of the business. The computer continues to function normally, while the hidden program is free to collect data, make secret modifications to programs and files, erase or destroy data, and even cause a complete shutdown of operations. Trojan horses can be programmed to destroy all traces of their existence after execution.

Salami Techniques: The perpetrator can make secret changes to the computer program that cause very small changes that are unlikely to be discovered, but whose cumulative effect can be very substantial. For example, the perpetrator may steal ten cents from the paycheck of each individual and transfer it to his own account.

Back Door or Trap Door: During the development of a computer program, programmers sometimes insert a code to allow them to bypass the standard security procedures. Once the programming is complete, such code may remain in the program either accidentally or intentionally. Attackers rely on their knowledge of this extra code to bypass security.

Time Bomb/Logic Bomb: A code may be inserted into a computer program that causes damage when a predefined condition occurs.

Masquerade: A computer program is written that masquerades or simulates the real program. For example, a program may be written to simulate the log-in screen and related dialogue. When a user attempts to log-in, the program captures the user's ID and password and displays some error message prompting the user to log-in again. The second time, the program allows the user to log-in and the user may never know that the first log-in was fake.

Scavenging: A computer normally does not erase data that is no longer needed. When the user "deletes" some data, that information is not actually destroyed; instead, that space is made available for the computer to write on later. A scavenger may thus be able to steal sensitive data, which the user thought had been deleted, but was actually still available on the computer.

Viruses: Viruses are similar to Trojan horses, except the illegal code is capable of replicating itself. A virus can rapidly spread throughout the system and eradicating it can be expensive and cumbersome. To guard against viruses, there should be care in using programs on diskettes or in copying software from bulletin boards or outside the company. Disks should only be used from verified sources. The best precaution is to use a commercial virus scanner on all downloaded files before using them. An example is McAfee's virus scan. Virus protection and detection is crucial.

Data Manipulation: The most common and easiest way of committing fraud is to add or alter the data before or during input. The best way to detect this type of computer crime is the use of audit software to scrutinize transactions and review audit trails that indicate additions, changes, and deletions were made to data files. The use of batch totals, hash totals, and check digits can also help prevent this type of crime. A batch total is a reconciliation between the total daily transactions processed by the computer and manually determined totals by an individual other than the computer operator. Material deviations must be investigated. A hash total is adding values that would not typically be added together so the total has no meaning other than for control purposes. Examples are employee and product numbers. A check digit is used to ascertain whether an identification number (e.g., account number, employee number) has been correctly entered by adding a calculation to the identification number and comparing the outcome to the check digit.

Piggybacking: Piggybacking is frequently used to gain access to controlled areas. Physical piggybacking occurs when an authorized employee goes through a door using his magnetic ID card, and an unauthorized employee behind him also enters the premises. The unauthorized employee is then in a position to commit a crime. Electronic piggybacking may also occur. For example, an authorized employee leaves his terminal or desktop and an unauthorized individual uses that to gain access.

Phishing or Spoofing (Fraudulent emails)

Fraudulent emails, also known as "Phishing" or "Spoofing", are unexpected emails that appear to be from a bank, insurance company, retailer or a regulatory agency, but they are not.

◆ These messages look professional and official, and may even contain links or pop-up windows that also have the appearance of legitimacy. View a sample of a fraudulent email.

◆ The fraudulent emails require you to "verify" certain information to prevent account suspension, closing or some other urgent matter.

◆ These sophisticated scams may ask for ATM or credit card numbers, PINs or log-on IDs and personal information such as Social Security Number, Date of Birth, or Mother's Maiden Name; all of which can be used by criminals to perform an account takeover or even worse, commit identity theft.

Tips to avoid becoming a victim are the following:

◆ Delete emails from unknown parties. Don't even open them.

◆ Use email (SPAM) filtering software.

◆ Do not provide personal information, account numbers, ATM, debit or credit card numbers, PINs or log-on IDs through email links or pop-up windows. Either call the institution, or go directly to their web site at the URL you know to be correct.

◆ NEVER give out any personal information unless you initiated the contact, and are sure you know with whom you are dealing.

Identity Theft

Identity theft is when someone pretends that they are you when committing a crime. Crimes involving identity theft or impersonation are on the rise and are now the types of crimes that are most frequently reported to the Federal Trade Commission. The crime could be in person, over the telephone or Internet, or through the mail.

The increase in identity theft is mainly attributable to technology. As technology continues to evolve, criminals are developing new ways to exploit or defraud organizations and consumers alike, including attempts to access bank accounts, brokerage accounts, and/or steal credit information or identities. Both state and federal governments continue to enact legislation to help protect consumers and banks is diligent in its efforts to protect customers' information

How You Can Help Prevent Identity Theft:

◆ Report any lost or stolen cards immediately.

◆ Pay attention to billing cycles and call if you do not receive an expected bill in a timely manner. It may mean that an identity thief has diverted the bill.

◆ Place outgoing mail in post office collection boxes only. Even better, consider using online banking with bill payment to send your payments. Making payments online can help prevent mail fraud while saving you time and postage.

◆ Shred all of your receipts and bank and credit card statements before disposing of them.

◆ Review your credit report from all three major credit bureaus to make sure that new credit card or other accounts have not been opened in your name. The three major credit bureaus to contact are Equifax (www.equifax.com/), Experian (www.experian.com), and TransUnion (www.transunion.com/).

◆ Make sure personal and financial information stored on your personal computers are protected with a password.

◆ Avoid using automatic login features that save your user name and password; and always log off when you're finished.

◆ Install and use a firewall on your personal computers, especially those connected to the Internet through high-speed DSL or cable modems. A firewall helps prevent hackers from accessing your computer.

◆ Install virus protection software on your computer and make sure it is updated on a regular basis.

◆ Don't give anyone your financial information unless you initiate the contact or are sure with whom you are dealing.

◆ Never disclose your PIN or password to anyone and always safeguard it.

◆ Don't print your Social Security number or driver's license number on your checks.

◆ Don't download files or click on hyperlinks in emails from un-trusted sources.

◆ Watch out for "phishing" or "spoofing" e-mails that may look like they are legitimate messages, but they are not. The sender attempts to get you to reveal confidential personal information that can be used for identity theft.

What to Do if You Are a Victim of Identity Theft:

◆ Notify your bank or financial institution at the phone number listed on your statement along with any other financial service providers.

◆ File a report of identity theft with your local police.

◆ Contact one of the three major credit bureaus to report the incident and ask to have a fraud alert placed on your file. Once the credit bureau confirms your fraud alert, the other two credit bureaus will be automatically notified to place fraud alerts, and all three credit reports will be sent to you free of charge. Review your credit reports and notify the bureaus about anything that looks suspicious.

Additional Identity Theft Resource Materials are available for download in PDF format to help you recover from Identity Theft, including instructions on how to complete an ID Theft Affidavit, related forms and sample letters. For additional valuable information about identity theft we recommend you visit **www.consumer.**

gov/idtheft/index.html or call 1-877-ID THEFT, the FTC's toll-free ID Theft Hotline.

Protect Your Company from Internet Dangers

1. **Have an external firewall.** A firewall is simply a device that prevents hackers from gaining access to your company network. For small companies, use a broadband router, like those made by Netgear, Linksys or D-Link, that has a firewall built in.

2. **Use an anti-virus program and keep it current.** Any of the popular brands will work (e.g. Norton, McAfee, etc.). Renew your subscription every year or upgrade to the latest version. Make sure that your computers are automatically getting the latest virus definitions.

3. **Get Microsoft Windows and Office updates.** Microsoft has introduced significant security improvements in Service Pack 2 for Windows XP that can be updated for free. Older versions of Windows are more susceptible to spyware and Internet worms. Consider upgrading PCs to Windows XP.

4. **Use anti-spyware and anti-spam programs.** Microsoft offers a free anti-spyware program for Windows 2000 and XP. Many Internet service providers (e.g., Cox Communications, AOL, etc.) offer complimentary anti-spam services. If your provider doesn't, there are spam filter programs that work with Outlook and Outlook Express.

5. **Secure your network.** A firewall won't protect you if a hacker can figure out the password. Make sure your computer technician has changed the default password on your router. If you have a wireless network, make sure it is using WEP or WPA encryption to prevent unauthorized access.

Considerations in Designing Networks

The architecture of a network includes hardware, software, information link controls, standards, topologies, and protocols. A protocol relates to how computers communicate and transfer information. Security controls must exist over each component within the architecture to assure reliable and correct data exchanges. Otherwise, the integrity of the system may be compromised.

In designing the network, one must consider three factors. First, the user should get the best response time and throughput. Minimizing response time entails shortening delays between transmission and receipt of data; this is especially important for interactive sessions between user applications. Throughput involves transmitting the maximum amount of data per unit of time.

Second, the data should be transmitted along the least-cost path within the network, as long as other factors, such as reliability are not compromised. The least-cost path is generally the shortest channel between devices and involves the use of the fewest number of intermediate components. Furthermore, low priority data can be transmitted over relatively inexpensive telephone lines, while high priority data can be transmitted over expensive high-speed satellite channels.

Third, maximum reliability should be provided to assure proper receipt of all data traffic. Network reliability includes not only the ability to deliver error-free data, but also the ability to recover from errors or lost data in the network. The network's diagnostic system should be capable of locating problems with components and perhaps even isolating the component from the network. *Note:* Public-switched networks are wide area networks that use public telephone lines. This arrangement may be the most economical, but data transmission may be of lower quality, no connection may be available, and security measures may be ineffective.

Network Media

The considerations in selecting a network medium are:

- Technical reliability
- Type of business
- Number of individuals who will need to access or update accounting data simultaneously
- Physical layout of existing equipment
- Frequency of updating
- Number of micros
- Compatibility
- Cost
- Geographic dispersion
- Type of network operating software available and support
- Availability of application software
- Expandability in adding additional workstations
- Restriction to PCs (or can cheaper terminals be used?)
- Ease of access in sharing equipment and data
- Need to access disparate equipment like other networks and main frames
- Processing needs
- Speed
- Data storage ability
- Maintenance
- Noise
- Connectivity mechanism
- Capability of network to conduct tasks without corrupting data moving through it

Network Topologies

The network configuration or topology is the physical shape of the network in terms of the layout of linking stations. A node refers to a workstation. A bridge is a connection between two similar networks. Network protocols are software implementations providing support for network data transmission. A server is a micro or a peripheral performing tasks such as data storage functions within a local area network (LAN). Network servers are of several types. A dedicated server is a central computer used only to manage network traffic. A computer that is used simultaneously as a local workstation is called a nondedicated server. In general, dedicated servers provide faster network performance since they do not take requests from both local users and network stations. In addition, these machines are not susceptible to crashes caused by local users' errors. Dedicated servers are expensive and cannot be disconnected from the network and used as stand-alone computers. Nondedicated servers have a higher price-performance ratio for companies that need occasional use of the server as a local workstation.

The most common types of network topologies are as follows:

◆ The hierarchical topology (also called vertical or tree structure) is one of the most common networks. The hierarchical topology is attractive for several reasons. The software to control the network is simple and the topology provides a concentration point for control and error resolution. However, it also presents potential bottleneck and reliability problems. It is possible that network capabilities may be completely lost in the event of a failure at a higher level.

◆ The horizontal topology (or bus topology) is popular in local area networks. Its advantages include simple traffic flow between devices. This topology permits all devices to receive every transmission; in other words, a single station broadcasts to multiple stations. The biggest disadvantage is that since all computers share a single channel, a failure in the communication channel results in the loss of the network. One way to get around this problem is through the use of redundant channels. Another disadvantage with this topology is that the absence of concentration points makes problem resolution difficult. Therefore, it is more difficult to isolate faults to any particular component. A bus network usually needs a minimum distance between taps to reduce noise. Identifying a problem requires the checking of each system element. A bus topology is suggested for shared databases but is not good for single-message switching. It employs minimum topology to fill a geographic area, while at the same time having complete connectivity.

◆ The star topology is a very popular configuration and it is widely used for data communication systems. The software for star topology is not complex and controlling traffic is simple. All traffic emanates from the hub or the center of the star. In a way, the star configuration is similar to the hierarchical network; however, the star topology has more limited distributed processing capabilities. The hub is responsible for routing data traffic to other components. It is also responsible for isolating faults, which is a relatively simple matter in the star configuration. The star network, like the hierarchical network, is subject to a potential bottleneck at the hub and may cause serious reliability problems. One way to minimize this problem and enhance reliability is by establishing a redundant back-up of the hub node. A star network is best when there is a need to enter and process data at many locations with day-end distribution to different remote users. Here, information for general use is sent to the host computer for subsequent processing. It is easy to identify errors in the system, since each communication must go through the central controller. Maintenance is easily performed if the central computer fails the network. There is a high initial cost in setting up the system because each node requires hookup to the host computer in addition to the mainframe's cost. Expansion is easy, as all that is needed is to run a wire from the terminal to the host computer.

◆ The ring topology is another popular approach to structuring a network. The data in a ring network flows in a circular direction, usually in one direction only. The data flows from one station to the next station; each station receives the data and then transmits it to the next station. One main advantage of the ring network is that bottlenecks, such as those found in the hierarchical or star networks, are relatively uncommon. There is an organized structure. The primary disadvantage of the ring network is that a single channel ties all of the components in a network. The entire network can be lost if the channel between two nodes fails. Establishing a backup channel can usually alleviate this problem. Other ways to overcome this problem is by using switches to automatically route the traffic around the failed node, or install redundant cables. A ring network is more reliable and less expensive when there is a minimum level of communication between micros. This type of network is best when there are several users at different locations who have to access updated data on a continual basis. Here, more than one data transmission can occur simultaneously. The system is kept current on an ongoing basis. The ring network permits accountants within the firm to create and update shared databases. With a ring, there is greater likelihood of error incidence compared to a star because numerous intervening parties handle data. In light of this, the accountant should recommend that data in a ring system make an entire circle before being removed from the network.

◆ The mesh topology provides a very reliable, though complex, network. Its structure makes it relatively immune to bottlenecks and other failures. The multiplicity of paths makes it relatively easy to route traffic around failed components or busy nodes.

LANs and WANs

The major differences in WANs and LANs means that their topologies usually take on different shapes. A WAN structure tends to be more irregular. Since an organization generally leases the lines at a considerable cost, an attempt is usually made to keep the lines fully utilized. To accomplish this, data is often routed for a geographical area through one channel; hence, the irregular shape of the WAN network.

The LAN topology tends to be more structured. Since the channels in a LAN network are relatively inexpensive, the owners of a LAN are generally not concerned with the maximum utilization of channels. Furthermore, since LANs usually reside in a building or a plant, such networks tend to be inherently more structured and ordered. LANs are flexible, fast, and compatible. They maximize equipment utilization, reduce processing cost, reduce errors, and provide ease of information flow. LANs use ordinary telephone lines, coaxial cables, fiber optics, and other devices like interfaces. Fiber optics result in good performance and reliability but are of high cost. LAN performance depends on physical design, protocols supported, and transmission bandwidth. Bandwidth is the frequency range of a channel and reflects transmission speed along the network. As more devices become part of the LAN, transmission speed decreases.

Two or more LANs may be interconnected. Each node becomes a cluster of stations (subnetworks). The LANs communicate with each other.

Advantages of interfacing networks include:

◆ Total network costs are lower.

◆ There is flexibility in having individual subnetworks meet particular needs.

◆ More reliable and higher cost subnetworks can be used for critical activities and vice versa.

◆ If one LAN fails, the other LAN still functions.

Disadvantages of interfacing networks include:

◆ Complexity is greater.

◆ Some network functions may not be able to go across network boundaries.

Communications Security

Communication systems are used to link data between two or more sites. The communication system should be reliable, private and secure. Communication systems are frequently affected by environmental factors, hardware malfunction and software problems.

Attacks on computers that do not require physical access fall under the domain of communications security. The increased use of computer technology has also increased dependence on telecommunications. All types of data, including sound, video, and traditional data, are transferred between computers over networks. Communications security means ensuring that the physical links between the computer networks function at all times. This also means that during data transmission, breakdowns, delays, and disturbances are prevented. Care must be taken to prevent unauthorized individuals from tapping, modifying, or otherwise intercepting data transmission. Six considerations in communications security are:

Line Security: Line security is concerned with restricting unauthorized access to the communication lines connecting the various parts of the computer systems.

Transmission Security: Transmission security is concerned with preventing unauthorized interception of communication.

Digital Signature: This is used to authenticate the sender or message integrity to the receiver. A secure digital signature process is comprised of (1) a method of signing a document making forgery infeasible and (2) validating that the signature is the one of whom it purports to be.

Cryptographic Security: Cryptography is the science of secret writing. The purpose of cryptographic security is to render the information unintelligible if transmission is intercepted by unauthorized individuals. When the information is to be used, it can be decoded. Encryption of sensitive data is necessary. A common method is the Data Encryption Standard (DES). For even greater security, double encryption may be used in which encryption is processed twice using two different keys. (One may also encrypt files on a hard disk to prevent an intruder from reading the data).

Emission Security: Electronic devices emit electromagnetic radiation which can be intercepted, without wires, by unauthorized individuals. Emission security is concerned with preventing the emission of such radiation.

Technical Security: Technical security is concerned with preventing the use of devices such as a microphone, transmitters, or wiretaps to intercept data transmission. Security modems may be used allowing only authorized users to access confidential data. A modem may have graduated levels of security. Different users may be assigned different security codes. There can be password and call back features. There may be built-in audit trail capabilities allowing you to monitor who is accessing private files.

Many companies are using Value Added Networks (VANs). VANs offer both communication services as well as specialized data processing. It is important to consider the security provided by VANs. Generally, a company has no direct control over a VANs' security. However, VANs' security has a direct effect on the client organization's overall security.

Communication security may be in the form of:

◆ *Access control:* Guards against improper use of the network. For example, KERBEROS is commercial authentication software that is added to an existing security system to verify a user's existence to assure he or she is not an impostor. KERBEROS does this by encrypting passwords transmitted around networks. Password control and user authentication devices may be used such as Security Dynamics' SecurID (800-SECURID) and Vasco Data Security's Access Key II (800-238-2726). Do not accept a prepaid call if it is not from a network user.

Hackers do not typically spend their own funds. Review data communications billings and verify each host-to-host connection. Review all dial-up terminal users. Are the telephone numbers unlisted and changed periodically? Control specialists should try to make unauthorized access to the network to test whether the security is properly working.

◆ *Identification*: Identifies the origin of a communication within the network such as identifying the entity involved through digital signals or notarization.

◆ *Data confidentiality*: Maintains confidentiality over unauthorized disclosure of information within the communication process.

◆ *Data integrity*: Guards against unauthorized changes (e.g., adding, deleting) of data at both the receiving and sending points such as through cryptographic methods. Anti-virus software should be installed at both the network server and workstations. Detection programs are available to alert users when viruses enter the system.

◆ *Authentication*: Substantiates the identity of an originating or user entity within the network. There is verification that the entity is actually the one being claimed and that the information being transmitted is appropriate. Examples of security controls are passwords, time stamping, synchronized checks, nonrepudiation, and multiple-way handshakes. Biometric authentication methods measure body characteristics with the use of equipment attached to the workstation. Retinal laser beams may also be used. Keystroke dynamics is another possibility for identification.

◆ *Digital signature*: Messages are signed with a private key.

◆ *Routing control*: Inhibits data flow to insecure network elements such as identified unsecure relays, links, or subnetworks.

◆ *Traffic padding*: A traffic analysis of data for reasonableness.

◆ *Interference minimization*: Radar/radio transmission interference must be eliminated or curtailed. There are various ways to backup data in networks. For a small network, one workstation may be used as the backup and restore for other nodes. In a large network, several servers may perform backups since the failure of one could have disastrous effects on the entire system. Access to backup files must be strictly controlled.

Token-Ring and Ethernet Networks

Traditional Token-Ring and Ethernet networks work on the broadcast principle. These networks send information in units called frames. Each frame contains information about a variety of items, including the sender's and the receiver's address. The sender broadcasts a frame that every receiver can see. At any given moment only one computer in the network is broadcasting and all other computers act as receivers. Another computer may broadcast after the first computer's broadcast is completed. While all machines on a network can see the broadcasting computer's frame, under ideal conditions, only the computer whose address matches the receiver's address in the frame should be able to access the frame's contents.

Sniffers

Sniffers are programs designed to capture certain information. Network managers frequently use sniffers to analyze network traffic and network statistics. Hackers, however, may use sniffers to steal information, such as passwords.

Taking certain actions can minimize sniffing risk. The most obvious solution is to limit access. If the hacker is unable to access the LAN, sniffers cannot be used. However, it is often possible to restrict access to networks too tightly; hence, other alternatives need to be considered.

Switched versions of token-ring and Ethernet networks may be used to minimize sniffing. With a switched LAN, each user has his own port on the switch. A virtual connection is established with the destination port for each frame sent. If destination address in the frame does not match, the risk associated with sniffing is significantly reduced. Switched networks tend to be more expensive. Moreover, it is rare to find completely switched networks.

Probably the best way to minimize sniffing risk is to use data encryption. In such a system, it is important that the key is never sent over the network. Traditional information, such as the time, is used to enhance the encryption scheme.

Data Flow

Data switching equipment is used to route data through the network to its final destinations. For instance, data switching equipment is used to route data around failed or busy devices or channels.

Routers at each site are used to communicate with routers at other sites. Routers provide information about the individuals and the resources available in the LAN. Routers are responsible for directing the flow of information. It is possible to configure the routers so that certain types of routers, such as FTP or telenet do not allow either incoming or outgoing access. It is also possible to enable or disable certain routers to receive information from only certain network addresses. Route and packet filtering requires significant technical knowledge as well as time. Most routers do not provide a security or audit trail. You need to know:

Who tried to break in to the computer system?

How frequently they tried?

What means and methods were used to attempt the break-in?

Data Transmission

Data transmission between computers in a network uses one of three methods:

◆ Simplex transmission is in one direction only. An example of simplex transmission is radio or television transmission. Simplex transmission is rare in computer networks due to the one-way nature of data transmission.

◆ Half-duplex transmission is found in many systems. In a half-duplex system, information can flow in both directions. However, it is not possible for the information to flow in both directions simultaneously. In other words, once a query is transmitted from one device, it must wait for a response to come back.

◆ A full-duplex system can transmit information in both directions simultaneously; it does not have the intervening stop-and-wait aspect of half-duplex systems. For high throughput and fast response time, full-duplex transmission is frequently used in computer applications.

Security Layers

Security should be provided in different layers. Security must exist over networking facilities and telecommunication elements. Controls must be placed over both host computers and subnetworks.

Network traffic may be over many subnetworks, each having their own security levels depending on confidentiality and importance. Therefore, different security services and controls may be required. Security aspects of each subnetwork have to be distributed to the gateways so as to incorporate security and controls in routing decisions.

Network Backup

Backup capability is an especially important feature of networks. For instance, if one computer fails, another computer in the network can take over the load. This might be critical in certain industries such as financial institutions.

Secure Sockets Layer

When *Secure Sockets Layer* (SSL) is enabled, a web browser will display a lock or another symbol to indicate that the data transfer is secure. Another way to tell that the web site is secure is by looking at its address: the web site address should start with "https://" rather than simply "http://." Most web-based monetary transactions are secured using SSL. Many web server/client products support SSL connections. To transact on the web, one needs access to such a server as well as a digital certificate. While using SSL for encryption greatly enhances security and confidentiality, it does slow the communication interchange. All the data has to be encrypted and then decrypted.

Secure Sockets Layer protocol was developed by Netscape. SSL operates by layering a security protocol on top of an underlying connection transport protocol such as HTTP, Telnet, NNTP, FTP and TCP/IP. SSL is built in to Netscape's client and server products. When building a web site, one can enable SSL by configuring a security-enabled http (https) process on the server. Web pages that require SSL access can be specified. Common Gateway Interface (CGI) routines can be written on the server side to integrate SSL into existing applications.

SSL provides data encryption and checks for data integrity. It provides server authentication, and if required, client authentication, for a TCP/IP connection. SSL is an open and nonproprietary protocol. Encryption, decryption and authentication are performed transparently for applications utilizing the SSL protocol.

SSL is used extensively to encrypt and authenticate communications on the World Wide Web (WWW) between clients and servers. The *Transport Layer Security* (TLS) standard by the Internet Engineering Task Force (IETF) is based on SSL.

A user can confirm and authenticate a SSL server's identity. Such confirmation is necessary when the user is sending sensitive information, such as a credit card number, to the server and wants to check the server's identity. The digital certificate serves as the key to SSL. It is used to prove authenticity. Certificate Authorities (CA) such as VeriSign Inc. issue digital certificates. Anyone with the correct software can become a certificate authority, but there are only certain trusted CAs that a web browser will accept. It is possible to tell the web browser which CA it should accept.

Public-key cryptography techniques may be used to check if a server's certificate and public ID are valid and were issued by a trusted CA. Similarly, a server can confirm a user's identity by checking that the client's certificate and public ID are valid and were issued by a trusted CA.

Public key cryptography greatly facilitates key management. Without public key cryptography, encrypted communication could take place between two or more users only if they shared the keys. The users need to maintain a secure connection to share the secret key. This means that each user would have to maintain several keys for communicating with various users.

Public key cryptography allows parties to communicate securely without sharing secret keys. Each party establishes a key pair: one private key and one public key. The public key is published and is available to all nodes on a network. The public key is used to encrypt messages to the node. The private key is used to decrypt the messages. It never leaves its node on the network.

Public key cryptography is used to create digital signatures and sign documents. The document is signed using the private key, but other users can verify the signature using the public key. The digital certificate consists of the name and other information

120

about the user along with the user's public key. A trusted certificate authority signs the information on the digital certificate and verifies the identity of a user. The following steps are typically taken:

A user creates a public/private key pair.

The private key is stored with the user.

The public key is given to a trusted authority.

The trusted authority creates a digital signature for the user and provides a digital certificate.

The digital certificate may be published or attached to messages being digitally signed by the user.

Other users may verify the signature and authenticate the user's identity using the digital certificate.

The *Transmission Control Protocol/Internet Protocol* (TCP/IP) provides the rules for transporting and routing data over the Internet. Protocols such as the HyperText Transport Protocol (HTTP) use the TCP/IP to carry out tasks such as displaying web pages. The SSL protocol runs in the middle between TCP/IP and other higher level protocols, such as HTTP. It runs above TCP/IP, but below the higher level protocols. SSL utilizes TCP/IP on behalf of the higher level protocols. This allows SSL-enabled clients and servers to authenticate themselves and makes an encrypted connection possible.

Confidentiality in a SSL connection is ensured through encryption. All information transported between the client and server is encrypted in a SSL connection. The sending software encrypts and the receiving software decrypts the data. SSL connection also provides assurance that the data has not been tampered with or altered in transit.

The "strength" of an SSL connection depends on the bit level. For example, 40-bit SSL connections tend to be rather weak, whereas a 128-bit SSL connection is extremely strong. 128-bits is approximately three hundred and forty septillion times (340,000,000,000,000,000,000,000,000,000) larger than 40-bits.

One hundred twenty eight (128)-bit encryption is only available for American and Canadian residents. It is presently illegal for US companies to export internationally anything above a 56-bit encryption. Software security companies are trying to overcome these export restrictions by developing encryption technology outside of the United States.

The SSL protocol includes two sub-protocols. The *SSL Record Protocol* defines the format that will be used for data transmission. The *SSL Handshake Protocol* determines how the record protocol will exchange data between a SSL server and a SSL client when the SSL connection is first established. It is used to either authenticate the server to the client, or the client to the server. It also allows the client and server to select from the various cryptographic algorithms or ciphers supported by both the client and the server.

Both public-key and symmetric key encryption is used by the SSL protocol. While symmetric key encryption tends to be faster, public-key encryption provides better authentication. Commonly used ciphers include:

Data Encryption Standard (DES) is a commonly used encryption algorithm. Triple DES applies DES three times and supports 168-bit encryption. Its key size makes it one of the strongest ciphers supported by SSL.

Digital Signature Algorithm (DSA) is used for authentication of digital signatures.

Key Exchange Algorithm (KEA) is used for key exchange.

Message Digest (MD5) algorithm.

RSA is a public-key algorithm used for authentication and encryption. RSA key exchange algorithm is used for SSL connections. It is one of the most frequently used ciphers.

Secure Hash Algorithm (SHA-1).

SKIPJACK. A classified symmetric-key algorithm used in FORTEZZA compliant hardware. The FORTEZZA encryption system is used by the U.S. government agencies for sensitive but unclassified data. FORTEZZA ciphers use the Key Exchange Algorithm (KEA) for SSL instead of the RSA key-exchange algorithm. FORTEZZA cards and DSA are used for client authentication.

The RSA public-key cryptography system is most prevalent in commercial applications. It provides encryption, decryption, digital signatures and authentication capabilities. Performance can suffer when using public key cryptography. Therefore, public key encryption is typically limited to digital signatures or encrypting a small amount of data. Symmetric key encryption, such as DES and RC2 and RC4, is typically used for encrypting bulk data.

The supported ciphers for both the client and the server can easily be enabled or disabled. During the handshake, the client and server determine the strongest common enabled cipher suite and it is used for the SSL connection.

Security administrators should decide which cipher suites to enable or disable. Administrators should consider the nature of the data, the need for confidentiality and security, and the speed of the cipher. The national origin of the parties is another consideration since certain ciphers may only be used within the USA and Canada. Thus, if an organization disables the weaker ciphers, it automatically restricts access to clients within the United States and Canada; an international client may access the server only if it has a special Global Server ID.

SSL Handshake

The following sequence of events typically takes place in an SSL connection:

The client provides the server with the client's SSL version number, cipher settings, and a variety of other communications related data.

The server provides the client with the server's SSL version number, cipher settings, and a variety of other communications related data.

The server certificate is sent. If necessary, the client's certificate is requested.

The client authenticates the server. If there is an error and the server cannot be authenticated, the client is warned that an encrypted and authenticated connection cannot be established.

The client creates a "pre-master" secret for the SSL connection and encrypts it with the server's public key. The encrypted pre-master is then sent to the server. The client may also sign and send data as well as its certificate to authenticate itself, if requested by the server.

The session will be terminated if the server cannot authenticate the client.

The server uses its private key to decrypt the pre-master secret and to generate the "master" secret. The client generates the master secret using the same pre-master secret.

Using the master secret, session keys are generated by both the client and the server. The session keys are symmetric and are used to encrypt and decrypt data. The keys are used to ensure that the data is not tampered with between the time that it is sent and the time that it is received, and that data integrity has not been compromised.

The SSL session begins once the SSL handshake is completed. Both the client and the server use the session keys to encrypt and decrypt data and to verify the data integrity.

Authentication

Both client and server authentication requires encrypting data with one key of a public-private key pair and decrypting it with the other key. For server authentication, the client encrypts the pre-master secret with the server's public key. The associated private key alone can decrypt the pre-master secret. This provides the client with reasonable assurance about the server's identity.

For client authentication, the client encrypts some random pieces of data using the client's private key. In other words, it creates a digital signature that can be validated using the public key in the client's certificate, only if the corresponding private key had been used. If the server cannot validate the digital signature, authentication fails and the session will be terminated.

SSLRef

SSLRef is an advanced software developer's tool-kit. Its purpose is to help developers provide security features in TCP/IP applications using the SSL protocol. ANSI C source code is provided for incorporation into TCP/IP applications. SSLRef may be downloaded for free for noncommercial use. While there are no license restrictions, there are export restrictions on SSLRef.

Kerberos

Kerberos is a network authentication protocol that uses secret-key cryptography. The Kerberos protocol is used in a client/server environment to authenticate the client to the server and the server to the client. After the authenticating client/server identity, Kerberos may be used to encrypt data. Kerberos does not send across any data that may allow an attacker to learn secret information and impersonate the user.

Kerberos is available for free in the form of source code from the Massachusetts Institute of Technology. It is also available in commercial software products from several vendors.

When a client accesses a network service, the client asserts to the server that it is running on behalf of an authorized user. Without authentication, there is virtually no security. With Kerberos authentication, the client proves its identity to the server.

In the traditional environment, a user's identity is verified or authenticated by checking the user's password during the login process. Password-based authentication has several drawbacks in the networked environment. The most critical problem is that hackers can intercept passwords sent across the network.

Without Kerberos authentication, the user would need to enter a password to access *each* network service. This is, at a minimum, inconvenient. Moreover, it still does not provide security when accessing services on a remote machine. Without encryption, it would be easy for anyone to intercept the password during transit. Kerberos eliminates the need to use passwords. Instead, a key is used to encrypt and decrypt short messages and provide the basis for authentication.

Kerberos uses a series of encrypted messages to prove that a client is running on behalf of a particular user. The client, to prove its identity, presents a ticket issued by the Kerberos Authentication Server. Secret information, such as a password, that only an authorized user would know, is contained in the ticket.

Kerberos is not effective against password guessing attacks. It is, therefore, essential for the user to select a good password. Otherwise, it may be possible for a hacker who intercepts a few encrypted messages to launch an attack by randomly trying passwords to see if the messages decrypt correctly. If a hacker is able to guess the password, he will be able to impersonate the user.

Kerberos assumes that the workstations or machines are reasonably secure and only the network connections are vulnerable to attack. A trusted path for passwords is required. For example, if the password is entered into a program containing a Trojan horse (i.e., the program has been modified to capture certain information),

Kerberos will not provide any protection. Moreover, if transmissions across the path between the user and the authentication program can be intercepted, Kerberos will be ineffective.

Both the user and the network service must have keys registered with the Kerberos Authentication Server. The user's key is derived from a user-selected password. The network service key is selected randomly.

A version of Kerberos called Bones is available for international users. The Bones version was created since the United States restricts export of cryptography. All the DES routines have been stripped from Bones. Many types of software used by the international community require Kerberos. Bones is used as a substitute to "trick" other software into believing that Kerberos is installed. International users can get Encrypted Bones or E-Bones, which does provide encryption.

To use Kerberos, a Kerberos principal must be established. A Kerberos principal is like a regular account on a machine. Certain information, such as the user name and password, are associated with each principal. The information is encrypted and stored in the Kerberos database. Kerberos is essentially transparent from the user's perspective. To be effective, Kerberos has to be integrated into the computer system. Kerberos protects only data from software that is configured to use Kerberos.

The Kerberos Authentication Server maintains a database of passwords or encryption keys. It is, therefore, critical to protect the server system. The server, if possible, should be physically secure. Ideally, the machine should be dedicated to running the authentication server. Access to the machine should be strictly restricted.

While Kerberos is freely available from MIT, it is not officially supported. Several companies have taken reference implementations from MIT and provide commercially supported products.

Each user's initial password has to be registered with the authentication server. The registration procedure depends upon the number of users. In person registration provides the best control if the number of users is small. Other procedures, such as using a login program on a trusted system, may be used when the number of users is large.

Several tools can enhance the security provided by Kerberos. One-time passwords generated by a device are particularly useful. Kerberos cannot protect against a hacker guessing or stealing user passwords. One-time passwords eliminate that problem. Commercial products are available that combine one-time passwords with Kerberos.

Vendors for Kerberos

The web sites for some vendors that sell or support Kerberos are as follows:

http://www.cybersafe.com

http://www.latticesoft.com
http://www.stonecast.net
http://www.wrq.com

Firewalls

Firewalls are frequently used to overcome some of the problems associated with route and packet filtering. The firewall is a buffer between an organization's internal network and the external world. It is possible to configure the network such that outgoing data may travel freely across the firewall but incoming data is restricted. It is also possible to configure it so that only email may go in and out the computer and no other type of communication is allowed to take place.

The purpose of a firewall is to allow authorized traffic and restrict unauthorized traffic. A firewall is used to control access between two networks. Some firewalls are more concerned about restricting unauthorized traffic while others place greater emphasis on permitting traffic. Senior management in an organization should play an integral part in determining the kind of access to permit or deny.

A firewall can be very restrictive and allow only email messages to go through. Other firewalls may block certain types of services that are known to cause problems. Most firewalls are configured to protect against unauthenticated interactive logins from external networks. Firewalls can also be configured to allow internal users unrestricted access to outside services, while preventing traffic from the outside to the inside.

Unlike dial-in modem connections, firewalls provide logging and auditing functions for security purposes. For example, security data may be obtained about the number of login attempts and password failures.

Firewalls can't protect against all types of attacks. Many organizations are overly concerned about threats from sources external to the organization. However, firewalls can't protect against internal threats. It is just as easy for internal users to steal proprietary data since they don't have to go through the firewall. Other routes to the corporate network, as well as threats from internal users should be considered, and firewalls should be one part of the organization's security plan.

While several firewall vendors are offering virus protection tools, firewalls are not very effective against protection from viruses. It is relatively easy to transfer virus files over the network and relatively difficult to protect and search for such viruses. A file could be mailed to an internal host, copied and executed, and in general, firewalls cannot protect against such attacks.

A virus can come from many sources, not only via transfers from the Internet. Virus protection should be a part of an organization's overall security plan. Steps should be taken to protect against viruses from all sources, and especially internal sources where floppy disks are exchanged. Virus scanning software should be installed on each machine and should run automatically when the machine is booted.

Firewall policies should consider the nature of the data to be protected. If the data require a very high level of security, the organization must assess whether the data should even be accessible via the Internet. With top secret data, it may be wise to isolate it from the main corporate network.

Setting up a Firewall

The cost of setting up a firewall can range from virtually free to several thousands, even hundreds of thousands of dollars. When selecting a firewall system, one should consider not only the initial setup cost, but also the cost of ongoing maintenance and support.

The organization must decide the level of access that will be granted through the firewall. At one end, the firewall may be set up to block all services except those that are absolutely essential to establish connection. At the other end, the firewall may simply be used for monitoring and audit purposes. Most organizations would not want to be at either extreme. The sensitivity of the data will determine an organization's stance. The organization should explicitly decide what services should be permitted, denied, or simply monitored.

There are two basic types of firewalls. *Network* level firewalls rely on the source/ destination addresses and ports in individual IP packets. Network level firewalls generally route traffic directly and require an assigned IP address. Network level firewalls are typically fast and transparent to users.

Application level firewalls typically act as hosts running proxy servers. A proxy server or an application gateway mediates traffic between a protected network and the Internet. Proxy servers are frequently used to prevent traffic from passing directly through networks. Greater logging or support for user authentication is provided.

Application level firewalls do not allow any traffic directly between the networks. They control access as well as log and audit traffic passing through them. While improvements have been made, the performance of application level firewalls may not be as good and they may not be as transparent to the user as network level firewalls.

Future firewalls will contain the characteristics of both network level firewalls and application level firewalls. Network level firewalls will keep better track of information that goes through them, and application level firewalls will become more transparent. The overall effect will be better performance with elaborate logging and auditing functions. Encryption of data passing through the firewall is becoming increasingly common. With encryption, an organization can have multiple points of connectivity with the Internet and not be as concerned about password or data sniffing programs.

127

Resources for Firewalls

Resources required to protect a site using a firewall are likely to vary considerably due to variations in traffic type and system load. System scalability is important and a faster CPU will not necessarily enhance performance. Sufficient RAM is critical for busy systems to provide adequate performance. A denial-of-service attack can be easily launched against a system with insufficient RAM. At the very least, the system will have a backlog.

Security of DMZ

DMZ or *demilitarized zone* of a firewall refers to the part of the network that does not belong to either the internal network or to the Internet. This is generally the area between the Internet access router and the bastion host. The bastion host is a system that has been fortified against attacks. It is the system on the network where an attack is expected. Bastion hosts may be part of the firewall.

Putting access control lists on the access router creates a DMZ. An access control list contains the rules that define which packets are permitted or denied passage. The access router connects an organization's internal network with the external Internet. An access router is a company's first line of defense against attacks from the Internet. Creating a DMZ allows only authorized services to be accessible by hosts on the Internet. Attackers often try to exploit the relationship between a vulnerable host and other more attractive items.

If a system has several services that mandate different security levels, one option is to divide the DMZ into several separate zones. The effects of a security breach can be minimized by putting together hosts with similar levels of risks. Hence, even if an attacker is able to exploit some bug and gains access, the attacker will be unable to launch an attack against the private network if the bastion hosts are on a separate LAN. This may occur, for example, when the attacker is able to gain access to the web server.

Most organizations do not secure their web servers as strictly and allow services for Internet users that entail certain risks. Unauthenticated users might be able to run CGI or other executable programs on the web server. While this might be reasonable for the web server, it is unacceptable to run such programs on a bastion host, where the entire security mechanism might be compromised.

Services should be split up not only by host but also by networks. The level of trust between hosts on the networks should also be limited.

An organization should use redundant components to achieve maximum security. A single failure, such as a software bug, should not compromise the entire security mechanism. Risk related to software bugs can easily be reduced by keeping up-to-date on software fix patches using products that have been around a while and are well known running only necessary services.

Organizational Policy

The organization must decide which services to permit and which services to deny. This depends, to a great extent, upon the focus of the function of the firewall. An organization may be primarily concerned with allowing access or the organization may be primarily concerned with maintaining security.

If the emphasis is on maintaining security, the organization may decide to block everything and allow access on a limited or case-by-case basis. This way the organization can focus specifically upon the security concerns of the products or services it wishes to permit.

When deciding the services to permit, one should consider:

What effect will allowing this service have on firewall security?

How does permitting the service affect firewall architecture?

Will an attacker be able to exploit an inherent weakness?

How well known is the service?

Is the protocol for this service well known and published?

Restricting Web Access Using Firewalls

An organization may want to restrict web access to prevent users from viewing sites not related to their work. An organization may also want to block access to sites it deems inappropriate. While firewalls may be used to block access, it is a difficult task.

It is relatively easy for individuals to find an alternate route to a blocked site. Site-blocking products are typically not effective and are easy to circumvent. For example, inappropriate web pages may be fetched through email. It is virtually impossible to block everything.

Denial of Service Attacks

Attackers sometime decide to launch denial of service attacks by crashing, flooding or disrupting the network or firewall. Due to the distributed nature of networks, it is virtually impossible to prevent such attacks. For time-critical jobs on the Internet, it is essential to have a contingency plan in case the network is attacked or its capability degraded.

Using FTP, Telnet, Archie, Gophers through Firewalls

FTP (File Transfer Protocol) is usually supported in firewalls by using either a proxy server or allowing connections to networks at a restricted port range. Sometime,

FTP can be achieved by allowing the users to download files via the Web. Telnet is generally supported using an application proxy. Configuring a router to permit outbound connections using screening rules can also support Telnet. Both Gopher and Archie can be supported through Web proxies.

Internet Sources for Firewall Information

The following are additional Internet sources for firewalls:

http://sunsite.unc.edu/LDP/HOWTO/Firewall-HOWTO.html

http://www.net.tamu.edu/ftp/security/TAMU/

http://www.cs.purdue.edu/coast/firewalls/

Pretty Good Privacy (PGP)

Pretty Good Privacy (PGP) can be used to encrypt email messages or digitally signed messages. Encrypting messages provides the user with privacy. If the encrypted email is intercepted, it will appear to be garbage to the unauthorized recipient. Digital signatures can be used when the content of the message is not secret, but the sender wants to authenticate his identity and confirm that he wrote the message. PGP has proven itself to be very effective at protecting electronic messages.

PGP relies upon a public key encryption scheme. Unlike conventional encryption schemes, with public key encryption, there is no need to have a secure channel over which to share the key. The encryption and decryption keys are different when using such a public key encryption scheme. The public key is used to encrypt the data. It is readily available to the public and is typically available in a public database. The decryption key is private. No one has access to it except the intended recipient.

PGP is available for free for non-commercial use. ViaCrypt PGP is available for commercial use and costs under $100. ViaCrypt PGP is available for commercial use primarily in the United States and Canada. For the international community, commercial versions of PGP are available from Ascom Systec AG (IDEA@ascom.ch).

To use PGP, one must have two key rings: a public one and a private one. The public key ring holds your public key as well as the public keys of people known to you. The private key ring holds the secret or private key or keys.

Public key encryption is much slower compared to conventional. PGP combines two algorithms, namely RSA and IDEA, to encrypt plain text. It is essentially impossible to break the encryption algorithm using brute force. For PGP's IDEA encryption scheme, currently a 128-bit key is required. Using the fastest current technology it would still take several trillion years to break the encryption scheme.

To launch a successful attack against such a scheme, an attacker must understand the mathematical transformation that takes place between plain text and cipher text. By understanding the mathematical transformation, an attacker might be able to successfully launch an attack. The complexity of the transformation makes it extremely difficult to solve the mathematical problem.

At present, PGP gives you three choices for key size: 512, 768, or 1024 bits. It is also possible to specify the number of bits for your key. As the key size increases, the encryption becomes more secure. The key size affects the program's running time during generation. A 1024-bit key takes approximately 8 times longer to generate than a 384-bit key. This is a one-time process and doesn't need to be repeated unless another key pair is generated. Only the RSA portion is affected by the key size during encryption. The main body of the message is not affected by the key size. Therefore, it is best to use the 1024-bit key size. Some versions of PGP allow key sizes up to 2048-bits. Generating such a key will require a considerable amount of time; it is, however, a one-time process. Individuals running certain versions of PGP may be unable to handle very large keys.

Each time PGP is run, a different session key is generated. This session key is used for IDEA. This enhances the security of PGP.

Using PGP, it is possible to apply a digital signature to a message. If a trusted copy of the sender's public encryption key is available, then it can be used to check the signature on the message. It is impossible for anyone else to create the signature without the secret key. This will also detect if someone has tampered with the message. A digital signature protects the entire message.

If the contents of a message are not secret, but it is essential to allow others to verify the authenticity of the sender, clear signing digital signatures may be used. Clear signing works only on text files, it does not work on binary files.

Key signatures are used to authenticate that the signature really belongs to the sender and not an impostor. If the sender's key is not available, but a trusted source has added his signature to the sender's key, then you may infer that you have a valid copy of the sender's key. A chain of trust may be established for several levels: A trusts B who trusts C, therefore A may trust C. PGP can be configured to specify the number of levels this chain of trust is allowed. One should be cautious when dealing with keys that are several levels removed from your immediate trusted source.

You may sign someone's key if you wish to inform others that you believe the key belongs to that person. Other people may rely on your signature to decide whether or not that person's key is valid.

A key signing party is used to get together various users of PGP. A key signing party's purpose is to sign keys to extend the degree of trust on the web.

If the secret key ring is stolen or lost, the key should be revoked. If a strong pass phrase had been used to encrypt the secret key ring, there is little chance of damage. Both the pass phase and the secret key ring are needed to decrypt a message. Using a backup copy of the secret key ring, a key revocation certificate may be generated and uploaded to one of the public key servers. Before uploading the revocation certificate, it is useful to add a new ID to the old key to inform others what your new key ID will be. Without a backup copy of the secret key ring, it is impossible to create a revocation certificate.

Public key servers are used to make available one's public key. Everyone can use the public database to encrypt messages for you. Although there are several public key servers, it is only necessary to send your key to only one of them. The key server will then send your key to other public key servers. Keys may be submitted or extracted using the following site:

http://pgp5.ai.mit.edu/

Further information about PGP may be obtained from the Internet from the following sites:

http://dir.yahoo.com/Computers_and_Internet/Security_and_Encryption/
PGP___Pretty_Good_Privacy/

http://www.pgpi.com/links/

http://web.mit.edu/network/pgp.html

Security Analysis Tool for Auditing Networks

Security Analysis Tool for Auditing Networks (SATAN) is a tool to help security administrators identify network security problems. SATAN was written by Dan Farmer and Wietse Venema. They explain that they wrote SATAN because computer systems are becoming more dependent on networks, and becoming more vulnerable to attacks via the same networks.

SATAN examines a remote host or set of hosts. It gathers information by remotely probing various services such as *finger*, or *FTP* provided by the host. Potential security flaws and bugs, such as incorrectly setup or configured network services or known system bugs are identified. SATAN's expert system may be used to further investigate potential security problems.

SATAN consists of several programs. Each program tests for a specific potential weakness.

Additional test programs may be added to SATAN by putting their executable file into SATAN's main directory; these programs must have the *.sat* extension. The entire SATAN package, including source code and documentation, is freely available via FTP from various sites.

Courtney

Courtney software is available for free on the Internet. Courtney may be thought of as the anti-SATAN. Courtney monitors attacks from SATAN. Using Courtney, if SATAN probes your system, it notifies you and gives you a chance to trace the probe. Courtney can be downloaded from:

   http://ciac.llnl.gov/ciac/ToolsUnixNetMon.html#Courtney

Vulnerability Testing Using Automated Tools

Security frequently gets compromised because controls are improperly used. Generally, it is not that controls are lacking or that the existing controls are weak, but that the controls are not appropriately configured. Most computer software, for example, comes with a default setting. If these settings are left unchanged, security may end up being compromised.

The existence of such controls gives management and users the false impression that their data is secure. They assume that the controls are properly configured and rely upon them. Many hackers exploit well-known security weaknesses. They rely on common errors made by system administrators, such as not configuring the system properly or protecting the system with the latest security patches.

While incompetence or lack of time or other resources certainly contribute to this problem, many administrators may make mistakes because of the nature of the computer systems. Most systems support a wide variety of services and the security mechanism must be flexible enough to meet the needs of a variety of users. The system administrator and users are given the power to enhance or degrade security based upon one's needs. This flexibility can often lead to security weaknesses.

Many automated tools are available to audit the computer system and report potential security weaknesses. Such automated tools can examine thousands of files on a multi-user computer system and identify vulnerabilities that can result from improper use of controls or mismanagement. Such vulnerabilities include poor passwords or failure to update software with security patches. Automated tools may test for adequate virus protection or for the ability to plant Trojan horses or worms.

Such automated tools are available commercially or may be developed in-house to suit an organization's specific needs. These tools typically analyze file content and file attributes to identify vulnerabilities. The automated tools are capable of quickly analyzing and testing thousands of files.

Automated tools for testing security vulnerability are different from automated tools that monitor activity or detect intrusion. Monitors and intrusion detection systems analyze activity as it occurs. Vulnerability testing tools, on the other hand, search for potential weaknesses that may allow an attacker to gain unauthorized access.

133

Standalone Systems

To identify vulnerabilities in a standalone system, automated testing tools analyze shared executable files. These tools examine a variety of controls such as access controls or controls that are used to configure the system. For example, if the access controls are compromised, a hacker may be able to masquerade as an authorized user. The configuration files and shared executable files may be used to plant a Trojan horse. Vulnerability testing tools are used to analyze files whose modification or disclosure would allow the hacker to circumvent system controls and gain unauthorized access.

Automated vulnerability testing tools may be used to examine the password and access system. The testing tools can check if the passwords are long enough. Short passwords can be guessed easily using brute force (trying all possibilities). These tools can also check to see if passwords are changed periodically. Passwords should have a limited life and the user should not be allowed to select any password in their password history file. Passwords should be protected and stored in an encrypted file.

To prevent the planting of a Trojan horse program, certain precautions should be taken. User start-up files should be protected from modification. Start-up files are often used to plant Trojan horses because the start-up files are always executed. Write access in a user's personal file space should be limited.

The audit trail should always be maintained. System configuration files and shared binaries must be protected against unauthorized modification. Automated vulnerability testing tools can check to see if modification privileges for system binaries are restricted to systems staff. System binary files should be reviewed for unexpected changes. Only system staff should be able to modify system start-up scripts. Secure defaults should be specified.

In a networked environment, computer systems generally share data and other resources. Security controls for access paths in networks can be reviewed using automated vulnerability testing tools. A network host will not only have the potential vulnerabilities of a stand-alone system, but also the vulnerabilities contained in the networked system. In a networked environment, a hacker could masquerade as an authorized user or another system. Many systems use remote authentication, where the local host relies upon the remote system to authenticate users.

Vulnerability Testing Techniques

Vulnerability tests may audit the system or launch a mock attack. The nature of testing may be passive or active and their scope may be defined as broad or narrow.

Active tests are intrusive and identify vulnerabilities by exploiting them. In contrast, passive tests examine the system to infer the existence of vulnerabilities. An authentication system may be tested using either active testing or passive testing. An active test may launch a dictionary attack or randomly try common or short passwords. If successful, it would log the results for review by security personnel. A passive test of the authentication system might check the protection of a password file. It may copy the password file, encrypt it, and compare encrypted strings. Both types of tests provide useful information. However, active tests are riskier than passive tests. Individual circumstances and professional judgment is required in selecting appropriate tests.

Vulnerability testing programs may be classified according to scope. Their focus may be narrow and they may examine only a single vulnerability or their focus may be broad and they may examine the entire system.

It is possible to use a series of single vulnerability tests to identify risks and vulnerabilities. While single vulnerability tests tend to be simple, they do not generally consider the complete security ramifications. The joint effect of lack of controls may not be revealed through such testing. Weaknesses in multiple controls may compound the effect of the vulnerabilities.

System vulnerability testing provides better information than a series of single vulnerability tests. It is easier to determine the total risk using a system's vulnerability test.

Conclusion

Computer networks play a dominant role in transmitting information within and between firms. A network is simply a set of computers (or terminals) interconnected by transmission paths. These paths usually take the form of telephone lines; however, other media, such as wireless and infrared transmission, radio waves, and satellites are possible. The network serves one purpose: exchange of data between the computers and/or terminals.

Encryption must be used any time sensitive or confidential information is transmitted. The open nature of the Internet network is such that anything can be read or snatched at many locations between the originating site and the destination site. Encryption should be used not only when transmitting data, but also when putting any secret or sensitive information on the Internet server.

Hackers frequently take advantage of common security holes to break in. For example, they may take advantage of a bug in a software package. It is essential to have the most current version of the software package. The most current version is likely to have the fewest bugs. Most software developers provide patches, which may be downloaded from the developer's web site. These patches frequently fix known security bugs.

Businesses need security for a variety of reasons. The most basic reason is that you don't want accidental or intentional modification of data. In a networked environment, many security problems exist for a business. The more connections that exist, the more complex the system, and the greater the likelihood of security being compromised.

Chapter 7
Security Policy

Security concerns have heightened in recent years. News stories about viruses and computer fraud dominate. Information technology (IT) managers have to decide how to protect information and computer technology.

A risk analysis should be performed in planning computer security policies and financial support. Computer security risks fall into one of three major categories: destruction, modification, and disclosure. Each of these may be further classified into intentional, unintentional, and environmental attacks. The threat comes from computer criminals and disgruntled employees who intend to defraud, sabotage, and "hack." It also comes from computer users who are careless or negligent. Lastly, the threat comes from the environment; an organization must protect itself from disasters such as fire, flood, and earthquakes. An effective security plan must consider all three types of threats: intentional attacks, unintentional attacks, and environmental attacks. What is the company's degree of risk exposure?

Financial Loss and the Cost-Benefit Criterion

The danger of financial loss to a company can be greatly reduced by increasing computer security. In all likelihood, not investing in appropriate security measures will prove to be far more expensive for a company than investing in the appropriate security measures. It would even be appropriate for a company to consider the cost of investing in computer security as a form of insurance.

The cost of security measures must always be compared with the benefits received. As Figure 1 illustrates, the optimal level of security expenditure is when the combined cost of security measures and financial loss is minimized. The law of diminishing returns clearly applies here. Additional expenditures on security measures beyond a certain point are not likely to be cost effective. While appropriate security measures can greatly reduce the likelihood of a financial loss, security measures by themselves cannot guarantee against every kind of damage and accident: a certain degree of risk will always have to be accepted.

The cost-benefit criterion dictates that a company formally assess the risks it faces. The following three questions must be answered by the organization:

◆ What type of threats may affect our organization?

◆ What is the probability that a threat will occur?

◆ What is the potential liability for each threat?

For each type of threat, expected loss may be calculated as follows:

$$Loss\ Expectancy = Probability\ of\ Loss\ x\ Amount\ of\ Loss$$

Figure 1: Security Measures And Financial Loss

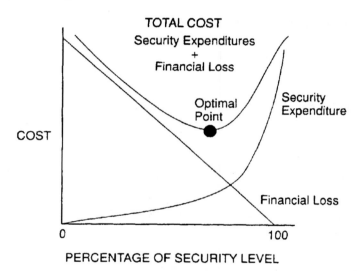

Using the above formula, expected losses may be classified into three categories. As shown in Figure 2, loss expectancy is highest for category (A) and lowest for category (C). Clearly considerable attention must be directed toward category (A) since there is both a high amount and a high probability of loss. In contrast, little attention needs to be given to category (C) items, which seldom occur and the associated loss is small. Professional judgment will be required to determine which items in category (B) require attention and which do not.

While the above model is theoretically appealing it does have serious practical limitations. The model relies heavily on estimating future probabilities and costs; it is extremely difficult to make such estimates with reasonable accuracy. When implementing the model, it is also possible for the user to overlook many serious indirect consequences of the threat.

Figure 2 Expected Loss Category

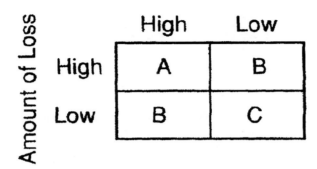

In developing a security policy, you must consider not only actual security threats but also the security perceptions of the public. For example, although it is in fact much safer to provide a credit card number over the Internet to a legitimate company than to give it to an unscrupulous employee in a face-to-face transaction, many people express concern about providing credit card numbers over the Internet. Not responding to the public's concerns may result in significant financial loss.

A manager you face several trade-offs concerning security management. While some may be quantified, others—such as determining the organization's strategic direction—cannot. That's why both the IT and the human resources department should be considered in formulating a security plan.

Without an adequate security policy, your organization is vulnerable to many threats:

- ◆ Theft of both electronic and physical resources, including data
- ◆ Unauthorized modification of data
- ◆ Fraud and other illegal activities
- ◆ Disclosure of confidential and proprietary information
- ◆ Unintentional errors caused by carelessness
- ◆ Intentional sabotage caused by current or former disgruntled employees
- ◆ Spying or sabotage by competitors
- ◆ Inability to continue business after an emergency or disaster

Managing Computer Security

In formulating a policy you must first ask yourself some questions:

1.   What resources need to be protected?
2.   Against whom must we protect our system?
3.   How much can we spend to protect the system?
4.   What benefits will we derive from the expenditure? Is the benefit worth the cost?
5.   What happens if security is compromised? How will we respond?
6.   What are our contingency plans?

Private, confidential, proprietary data is typically one important resource you want to protect. Otherwise, your financial assets might be compromised. Other valuable resources include CPU processing cycles or computer time. While attackers are typically interested in obtaining access to confidential data, some may simply want to deny legitimate users access to computer facilities.

Even information not likely to be valuable to anyone else should be protected. Hackers often steal or destroy data simply because it's there. They may also delete or destroy files in an attempt to cover up illegal activity.

When you're calculating the cost of security precautions, consider not only the direct but also the indirect costs. Direct costs may be for equipment, installation, and training. Indirect costs include the effects on morale and productivity.

It's prudent to recognize that increasing security decreases convenience. Employees and others, such as customers and suppliers, may resent the inconvenience. Too much security may be just as detrimental as too little; the goal is an optimal equilibrium.

In spite of precautions, security will eventually be compromised. The steps you take to recover from such a breach may mean the difference between success and failure in your business. Think about such questions as the following:

◆ What will be the financial impact of a security breach?
◆ Do you have enough insurance?
◆ What may be the legal consequences of a breach?
◆ How will lost data, information, or assets be recovered?
◆ How will the breach affect employees, suppliers, or customers?
◆ How can similar events be prevented in the future?

Creating the Policy and the Plan

The purpose of a security *plan* is to assign accountability. The security *policy* should define what is and is not acceptable.

The plan should clearly specify the penalties for unacceptable behavior. How will you reprimand violators inside the organization? How will you deal with violators outside? What type of civil or criminal action might you take?

The security policy should be integrated with your company's other policies and plans. For example, think about the internal control structure. Plan for contingencies. Make sure all your plans comply with the laws.

The role of the information systems department should be specified in the policy document. The department should be responsible for among other things, ensuring that security personnel are adequately trained and properly qualified. IS security personnel should be able to assist other departments with their security needs. Other responsibilities of security personnel might include:

◆ Assisting in acquiring hardware or operating systems

◆ Managing security of the communications networks

◆ Establishing standards for remote access

◆ Installing and maintaining virus detection software

◆ Selecting cryptographic techniques and keys

◆ Backing up critical data

◆ Evaluating and approving IS-related contracts

The Security Policy

The security policy should be a broad statement that guides personnel and departments in achieving certain goals. It should be concise and easy to read. It should not specify actions. The purpose of the security policy is not to educate or train individuals. That should be provided for in manuals and seminars.

The security policy, then, is written at a broad organizational level. The standards, guidelines, and procedures go into supporting documents. Some questions the policy should answer are:

◆ Why is it important to have a security policy?

◆ What is the meaning of data integrity?

◆ Why must data integrity be maintained?

◆ Why should data be kept confidential?

◆ What are the consequences to the organization if data is unavailable or compromised?

Standards, Guidelines, and Procedures

Standards, guidelines, and procedures provide the guidance the members of your organization need to realize the goals defined in the policy document. They give people clear instruction on how to meet organizational goals. *Standards* and *guidelines* specify the technologies and methodologies that may be used; *procedures* offer more detailed guidance to achieve particular security objectives.

All three should be published in handbooks, regulations, or manuals, both physical and electronic, as on the corporate Intranet or on CD-ROM. Providing the information in an electronic format has several advantages, among them easy access. It also makes it easier for you to keep the information current.

The purpose of *standards* is to specify a uniform set of technologies or procedures. Standards are typically mandatory; users may not exercise their own discretion in the areas they cover.

Guidelines, on the other hand, are provided because it's not always possible, appropriate, or cost-effective to impose standards. Guidelines give users some latitude in meeting goals. Guidelines are used to ensure, for example, that specific security measures are not overlooked. Guidelines inherently recognize that security measures may be correctly implemented in more than one way.

Procedures offer step-by-step guidance in adhering to standards and guidelines.

Buy-in

If you want your security policy to be effective, solicit participation from across the organization, both individuals and departments. Senior management's support is essential. You must provide the resources, financial and otherwise, to implement the policy adequately.

At the same time, users are far more likely to accept security policy, guidelines, and procedures if they had input in creating them. Their participation will help you create a better policy plan. The specialized knowledge each brings will result in a superior document.

Set up a senior management committee (the Information Security Management Committee) with authority to issue and amend the security policy. Make sure that people get from that committee approval for any exceptions to the security policy.

Scope

Your computer security policy should apply to all facilities and locations of the company. The same set of standards should be enforced throughout the company. While it's essential that security standards be applied consistently, they should be flexible enough to be used in a variety of situations.

Your security policies should encompass all types of computer systems, including stand-alone PCs, LANs, WANs, the Internet, and the Intranet. They should cover all types of data transmission, including email, FTP, and fax.

Risk Analysis and Management

Computer security planning is an integral part of your organization's overall risk management strategy. Each individual's and each department's responsibility should be clearly identified in the security plan, which should be updated regularly to meet changes in technology or circumstances.

You must therefore do a thorough risk analysis. Computer security risks fall into five major categories:

1. Destruction of data or equipment
2. Theft of data or equipment
3. Malfunction of equipment or bugs in software
4. Modification of data
5. Disclosure of data

The cause of risk may be:

◆ Intentional attack
◆ Unintentional or accidental loss
◆ Environmental threat

Intentional threat comes from computer criminals and disgruntled employees setting out to defraud, sabotage, alter data, or steal equipment or data. *Unintentional* loss may result from computer users who are careless. *Accidental* loss may be due to equipment malfunction. *Environmental* threats include fires, floods, earthquakes, lightning, and power outages. An effective security plan must cover all these threats.

Take out insurance policies to cover such risks as theft, fraud, intentional destruction, and forgery. Don't forget business interruption insurance, which covers lost profits and additional expenses during downtime.

Your risk analysis should take into account not only the security but also the reliability of your system; this can be compromised by errors, failures, and faults. An *error* is a deviation from expectations. Some errors are acceptable because they can be overcome; others are simply unacceptable. An unacceptable error is a *failure*. If the failure can have serious consequences, it's considered a *critical failure*. A *fault* is a condition that results in a failure.

It's important to note, however, that system reliability is conceptually distinct from system security. The purpose of computer system security is to protect against intentional misuse. System security doesn't really consider malfunctions or bugs unless they will allow a perpetrator to breach security. Still, improving one factor will typically enhance the effects of the other. That's why both security and reliability should be considered in managing risk.

The Security Administrator

The security administrator is responsible for customizing security policies and standards to the organization and for the planning, execution, and maintenance of the computer security system. The administrator should regularly interact with other departments to learn of their changing needs. Both technical computer knowledge and management skills are therefore necessary attributes for the security administrator, as well as a thorough understanding of the organization's internal control structure.

Specific aspects of an organization, such as its size and inherent risks, have to be taken into account in setting up the security administration department. The department must ensure the information systems data is reliable and accurate. Members of the department should keep abreast of organization requirements in dynamic environments to keep the security system efficient while monitoring staff to ensure compliance with policies. It is particularly important for you to have in place specific procedures for hiring and recruiting staff for this department (see Chapter 5).

The Human Factor

Typically, security systems depend more on people and their attitudes toward security than on the latest technology. Typically, too, the greatest security threat in an organization comes not from outsiders but from insiders. Personnel incompetence, indifference, and negligence are likely to cause more harm than sabotage or intentional acts by unauthorized hackers.

Security policies and procedures often conflict with people's ideas of good manners. Trusting others and sharing things with them is viewed positively. Security policies, on the other hand, require that you distrust others and not share information. For example, it's normally considered polite to hold a door open for someone behind you. However, in a restricted area, such politeness will result in a security breach. Similarly, sharing user I Ds or passwords may allow an unauthorized individual to access sensitive information.

Psychological Factors I

To make sure the people in your company accept the security policy, M.E. Kabay, director of education for the National Computer Security Association, recommends:

- ◆ Before attempting to implement policies and procedures, build up a consistent view of information security among your colleagues.
- ◆ Introduce security policies over time; don't rush them into place.

◆ Present case studies to help get people ready to accept security requirements.

◆ Give your people many realistic examples of security requirements and breaches.

◆ Inspire a commitment to security rather than merely describing it.

◆ Emphasize improvement effects rather than failure reduction.

◆ Explore the current beliefs of employees and managers.

◆ Don't portray computer crime with any positive images or words.

◆ Praise comments that are critical of computer crime or that support the security policies.

◆ Challenge rather than ignore employees who dismiss security concerns or flout the regulations.

◆ Identify the senior executives most likely to set a positive tone for security training.

◆ Immediately couple frightening consequences with effective and achievable security measures.

◆ Present objections to a proposal and offer counter-arguments rather than giving a one-sided diatribe.

◆ Make sure repeated novel reminders of security issues are part of your security awareness program.

◆ Include small gifts in your security awareness program.

◆ Find a charismatic leader to help generate enthusiasm for better security.

◆ Encourage specific employees to take on public responsibility for information security within their work groups.

◆ Rotate the security role periodically.

◆ Incorporate into your security training information on how to tell when someone may be engaging in computer crime.

◆ Build a corporate culture that rewards responsible behavior such as reporting security violations.

◆ Develop clearly written security policies and procedures.

◆ Be sure your security procedures make it easy to act in accordance with security policy.

◆ Emphasize the seriousness of failing to act in accordance with security policies and procedures.

◆ Enforce standards of security so that employees will later follow the standards more rigorously.

◆ Create a working environment in which employees are respected; this is more conducive to good security than one that devalues and abuses them.

◆ Have security supervisors get to know the staff.

◆ Encourage social activities in the office.

◆ Pay special attention to social "outliers" during training programs. Some people devoid of personal ethics can be very charming, sociable and still basically fundamentally dishonest.

◆ Monitor compliance closely to security requirements.

◆ Work with the outliers to resist the herd's anti-security bias.

◆ Before discussing security at a meeting, have one-on-one discussions with participants.

◆ Remain impartial; encourage open debate in security meetings.

◆ Bring in experts from the outside when faced with anti-security groupthink.

◆ Meet again after a consensus has been reached and play the devil's advocate.

Seminars

The importance of computer security must be instilled in all employees. Direct communication is typically more effective at persuading individuals than mass media like videos or books. Personalized messages stimulate thought and are likely to be more persuasive. An excellent way to both indoctrinate new employees and update the skills of current employees is to periodically schedule security seminars. Security professionals can communicate your company's rules and procedures at these seminars, as well as answer questions and address the security needs of employees.

Assign senior executives who are liked and respected to lead the seminars. A speaker's attractiveness and social status have an immediate effect on the audience. For a few days, the speaker's personal characteristics will continue to influence the audience, though the effect typically declines with the passage of time until only the message remains with the audience. The speaker should understand security issues and honestly believe in the policies he or she is advocating.

In trying to persuade employees, it's useful to present a balanced view, especially when trying to convince those who initially disagree with your policy. By presenting both sides of the argument you show your audience that you understand their perspective and have sound reasons for your own.

Other Communication Channels

Lecturing employees for a few hours per year, however, is unlikely to lead to improved security by itself. People need time to accept and acclimate to change; that's why new security policies should typically be phased in over time.

Repetition of the security message is helpful in building support for security policies. Security awareness may be enhanced with mugs, posters, and newsletters. Ongoing activities will yield better results than occasional training seminars alone, necessary though these are.

Videos and case studies containing examples of security breaches can have a beneficial effect. Exposing individuals to different security scenarios helps increase their awareness of security issues. Humans are not good intuitive statisticians. Intuitive human judgment is often prone to bias. Judgment is easily distorted when individuals tend to rely on small samples, easily available data, and personal anecdotal experience.

The use of questionnaires, focus groups, and interviews, may serve several purposes. They can help you obtain useful information about employees. They may also help to modify employees' beliefs, leading to a greater commitment to security. If you publicly support enhanced security, employees will change their perceptions and be more committed to security. When they take responsibility openly, their commitment to the task increases.

Behavior Modification

You can modify employee behavior by rewarding employees who support security policies and punishing those who do not. The reward may be as simple as verbal praise. The punishment may be a simple verbal warning, disciplinary action, or even removal from the job. Employees who flagrantly violate security policies should certainly hear about it.

The use of fear to change the attitudes of employees works only in certain situations. Too much fear about catastrophic consequences is likely to result in employees rejecting the message. When you tell employees about catastrophic consequences, also show them how to counter threats.

Account Administration

New users are continually being added to your system while old users must be deleted. Establish a written procedure for requesting, creating, maintaining, and closing user accounts. The purpose of account administration is to ensure that:

- The user is authorized.
- The user has access privileges appropriate to the job.
- The user is not engaged in unauthorized activities.
- Information about the user is current.

The user's supervisor should initiate the account creation process by requesting an account from the systems manager. The request should specify access level and the applications to which the user should have access. The approval of an applications manager may be required before the systems manager grants access to a particular application.

The user access level should be part of the account profile. Specific applications may have built-in access controls or may rely on third-party software for access control. The systems manager must ensure that a user's access is consistent with the request from the supervisor.

On being issued the user account and password, employees should undergo security training. At the very least, users should be provided with the written rules and guidelines and be required to sign an " account assignment" document indicating their understanding of those rules and guidelines. The document may be used to discipline or even prosecute users who violate them.

There are two techniques for creating user account IDs. The ID could be for a specific job title (SALESREP4) or for a specific employee (JACK_BLACK). From an auditing perspective, job title IDs simplify the process. However, if the account ID is for a specific job title, you'll need controls to ensure that the password is changed as soon as the employee changes job or leaves.

The user's supervisor should notify the systems and applications managers when a user is reassigned or the account is no longer required. The personnel department should also be required to notify those managers when there's a change in personnel or duties.

Access level privileges change. The change might be temporary or permanent. An employee may be temporarily performing the duties of another employee who is sick or on vacation. An employee may also be permanently assigned a different function or transferred to another department.

When an employee takes on additional duties during the absence of another employee, take care to ensure that he or she is not performing incompatible duties. From a control perspective, no one should be in a position to perpetrate an irregularity and cover it up in the normal course of the day. Temporary access privileges should also be removed as soon as they are no longer needed.

User accounts should be reviewed regularly to help detect unauthorized or illegal activities. The review may be of a sample of user accounts or the entire system. The level of access of each user should also be reviewed. Make sure that all new accounts have supervisory approval, and that the level of access granted is warranted by the job responsibilities.

Check that the accounts of all personnel who left the organization or were reassigned were properly closed, comparing data from the personnel department and the system manager's records.

Examine account records to assure that all users signed a statement acknowledging their understanding of rules and guidelines and that they have taken security awareness training.

For certain functions, periodic screening checks of personnel may be warranted. For example, an individual living a lifestyle considerably in excess of income is a red flag; it may be the fruit of fraudulent activity. The individual may be stealing corporate assets or giving competitors proprietary information.

Review the controls over account management during an audit and check compliance with controls. Just because a control exists doesn't mean users are actually following it.

One important control we have already mentioned is segregation of duties so that the employee cannot commit and conceal an illegal activity in the normal course of duties. Mandating that employees take vacations is also important from a security perspective. Some fraudulent activities require the perpetrators to take certain actions on a regular basis to prevent the fraud from being discovered.

In addition to mandatory vacations, you may want to rotate job assignments periodically. This serves the same purpose: It prevents a perpetrator from covering up illegal activities. Rotating job assignments has other benefits: When several individuals are trained to perform a single function, the organization is not excessively dependent on any single employee.

Conclusion

The primary benefit of the computer security policy is to prevent or minimize the loss of assets or resources due to a security breach. The document also provides a decision-making framework for purchasing software and hardware. It gives guidelines for steps to take after a security breach to prevent further breaches or losses.

A formal risk assessment should be part of the document. Assets to be protected, threats to those assets, and safeguards for those assets should be analyzed.

The rights and obligations of the users should be specified, along with rules for account use. Conditions that apply to personal users as well as public access accounts should be detailed. The document should also include criteria of acceptability of user software along with data access and use policies.

Users should be specifically warned against disclosing their passwords or other information that could potentially threaten the computer system. Privacy policies, including those applying to disclosure of confidential information to third parties, should be prominent, with special attention to user privacy, including conditions when the company may access a user's files.

The security policy should state what will happen if there is a security breach. It should answer questions like:

◆ If a security breach is in progress, who should be notified, and how?

◆ What audit trail must be maintained? What log files should be kept?

◆ How will the affected computer system or network be identified and isolated?

◆ What are the legal ramifications of entrapment? When must security officers identify themselves? *Note:* Entrapment is the act of luring into performing a previously or otherwise uncontemplated illegal act.

◆ How will violators be punished?

◆ When will law enforcement authorities be notified?

◆ How will the organization recover from a security breach?

Note: 10 keys to protecting personal information on computers at work:

1. Install and maintain a firewall to protect data.

2. Require all systems connected to your network to be configured safely.

3. Monitor security patches and keep them up-to-date.

4. Protect stored and transmitted data using encryption.

5. Use and regularly update antivirus software at gateways on personal computers.

6. Assign a unique ID to each person with computer access and track all access to data by that ID.

7. Ensure all system administrators have proven security skills.

8. Restrict physical access to data.

9. Implement and enforce an information security policy.

Source: The SANS Institute and VISA USA Inc.

Chapter 8

Contingency Planning

The purpose of computer security is to protect the information services of the organization as a whole. Information should not be lost, damaged, or modified. It should be readily available to authorized users. It should not be possible to accidentally or intentionally disable the computer system.

Contingency planning is a strategy to minimize the effect of disturbances and to allow for timely resumption of activities. The aim of contingency planning is to minimize the effects of a disruption on your organizations. A disruption is any security violation, man-made or natural, intentional or accidental, that affects normal operations. Disruptions in computer processing can be classified into three categories:

- ◆ **Malfunction:** *Minor disruptions that affect hardware, software, or data files. They're usually quite narrow in scope, and it's usually possible to recover from them quickly.*

- ◆ **Disasters:** *Disruptions to the entire facility. They typically require the use of alternate off-site processing facilities to recover operations. Entire facilities may be disrupted for a significant period of time.*

- ◆ **Catastrophes:** *The most serious type of disruption. In a catastrophe, the facilities may have been destroyed. Alternate facilities are always needed to process data. It may be necessary to rebuild or establish new or permanent facilities.*

Rarely will a company face either a disaster or a catastrophe. Malfunctions or other minor failures are likely to be the norm. For minor malfunctions, it's generally more convenient to use onsite backup facilities.

Your contingency plan should focus on the continuity of your business. Its primary purpose is to reduce the risk of financial loss and enhance your organization's ability to recover from a disruption promptly, at least cost. It should apply to all facets of your organization: staff, computer programs, data, workspace, production, and vital records. Contingency planning for your information systems should look at all critical areas including LANs and WANs, client server systems, distributed databases, and PCs.

A common mistake in contingency planning is an excessive focus on *computer* recovery. You really need a *business* recovery plan. Undue emphasis on the technology, rather than the business, is counter-productive. Quick recovery of computer technology is useless if your organization cannot recover its business. Excessive focus on computer technology results in committing too many resources to redundant processing facilities.

A contingency is an event that may or may not occur. The focus of computer security contingency planning is to provide options in case disruption strikes. Recovery from loss of key personnel is usually accomplished through succession planning and backup training. Computer facilities are typically covered by insurance policies and businesses can generally recover their investment in computers and equipment.

But losses in a disaster or catastrophe typically exceed what's recoverable through insurance policies. Some types of losses are uninsurable.

The primary focus of computer security should always be preventive rather than corrective action, though it's impossible to anticipate every problem; even if a problem can be anticipated, the cost/benefit ratio may not justify taking preventive measures. Sometimes precautionary measures may prove ineffective because of human or other error. Productivity and efficiency may also be sacrificed if precautionary measures are taken too far.

You'll need emergency procedures for each type of potential disaster. Think about how the disaster might affect data processing and business operations. How long would the service be interrupted? At what level would the company be able to operate?

Organizations are sometimes hesitant about using resources to develop a disaster or catastrophe recovery plan. The probability of a disaster or catastrophe is generally low, and the high costs associated with developing a detailed contingency plan may be a deterrent. Many organizations may feel that the costs exceed the potential benefits.

Yet while the probability of a disaster or catastrophe may be low, the cost of being unprepared is high. Most businesses are heavily dependent on computer technology; even a minor interruption could have serious financial consequences.

Contingency planning should provide an organized way to make decisions if there's a disruption. Its purpose is to reduce confusion and enhance the ability of the staff to deal with the crisis. When a disruption occurs, a company doesn't have the time to deliberate, plan, and organize its recovery. The organization needs to recover quickly. A well-tested, comprehensive recovery plan can save critical time (and therefore money).

The Role of Senior Management

Senior management has ultimate responsibility for establishing, regulating, and monitoring contingency plans. Senior management support is essential. Management must be willing to commit adequate resources, both tangible and intangible. The people at the top should appoint a team to manage the contingency planning process.

Top management has a fiduciary responsibility to protect the organization's assets. If after a disruption there are losses that could have been prevented or minimized by planning, shareholders and creditors may hold senior managers as well as the board of directors personally liable.

Government regulations, such as the Foreign Corrupt Practices Act of 1977 (FCPA), may impose additional civil and criminal penalties. The FCPA requires all publicly held organizations to maintain adequate controls over their information systems. Organizations may take reasonable steps to ensure the integrity of their records and the internal control structure. An organization that fails to protect its information records can be held in violation of the FCPA; penalties range from fines to imprisonment.

The Contingency Planning Committee

A committee should formulate, test, and implement your contingency plans; the information systems manager should be a key member, along with members from functional areas throughout the organization. The committee defines the scope of the plan, which should deal with how to:

◆ Prevent disruptions

◆ Minimize loss if a disruption cannot be prevented

◆ Recover from a disruption in an organized and expedient manner

The planning committee should consult with all major departments and specialists within and outside the organization before drafting a plan. Then each department should review the draft to suggest improvements and modifications. There's plenty of expertise to call on:

◆ *Internal auditors* will play a key role in evaluating the internal control structure and conducting operational audits. They are also familiar with the needs of external auditors.

◆ *The lawyers* should be consulted with respect to the legal consequences of a disruption, including compliance with government regulations, such as the FCPA.

◆ *The accounting and finance departments,* which are heavily dependent on information technology, are likely to suffer considerably from a disruption.

◆ *The security department* is responsible for coordinating the recovery efforts if there is a security breach, fire, earthquake, flood, or bomb threat.

◆ *Medical specialists* should be consulted for ways to protect human life in a disaster. They should know the effects of fire extinguishers, such as Halon or carbon dioxide, and other chemicals. They can advise on the type of first aid equipment that should be kept available and how employees should be trained.

◆ *The public relations department* should be responsible for all communications to the press and others outside the organization.

Areas to Cover

Human Safety

The primary concern in any type of planning should be the health and safety of the people who work for and with you. You need a plan for:

◆ Emergency evaluation

◆ Alerting the fire department and other emergency response authorities

◆ Health and safety concerns unique to the business (such as in a chemical manufacturing plant)

Business Impact Analysis

In formulating your disaster recovery plan, conduct a business impact analysis, determining the likely cost of each risk taken to a worst-case scenario. A business impact analysis considers how various threats and vulnerabilities might affect the continuity of your business. Incorporate into your plan recovery strategies for specific disasters, emphasizing your backup strategy, including the role of any off-site facilities that will be needed. Appendix 8.A contains an Impact Analysis Worksheet to help you with this.

Legal Liability

The planning committee may not realize the existence of certain liabilities during its risk analysis. The plan itself may violate certain legal requirements, exposing the organization to unnecessary liabilities.

To avoid that, the committee will need to review corporate documents, including the Articles of Incorporation and the by-laws, and then consider the impact of federal, state, and local laws on your contingency planning. Violation of laws may prevent recovery from insurance policies.

For example, the Worker Adjustment and Retraining Notification Act limits the right of an employer to lay off personnel or close a plant. Employers must provide at least 60 days notification to state and local officials as well as to employees. While natural disasters such as earthquakes are excluded from the notification requirement, other disasters-such as fires-are not. Without adequate insurance coverage, your organization may be unable to lay off personnel and must continue paying salaries and benefits to the remaining personnel.

Flexibility

The recovery plan has to be flexible enough to cover a wide variety of disasters and catastrophes. When planning for resources, consider the effects on your business of a single disaster, such as a fire, versus the effects of a community-wide disaster, such as an earthquake or flood. In a community-wide disaster, outside resources to help your organization may be severely strained. In your contingency planning, identify the resources you will need in both types of disasters.

Notification Procedure

The notification procedure in a disaster should be clearly specified. Ask yourself:
- ◆ Who should be notified?
- ◆ How are they to be notified? What if phone lines and e-mail aren't working?
- ◆ What mobile communications equipment might be needed to provide notification?
- ◆ Who will be responsible for notification?
- ◆ Where will the primary notification list be kept? Where will the backup list be kept?
- ◆ How often should the notification list be updated?

Access to Facilities

The recovery plan has to consider the effect of delayed access to facilities after a disaster. For example, even if a fire has been put out, the authorities may not allow anyone inside the building until they've assessed the amount of structural damage. Law enforcement authorities may be conducting a criminal investigation (e.g., arson), so the building may be considered a crime scene. In a manufacturing plant there may be danger of toxic chemical contamination. In a community-wide disaster like a tornado or a flood you may not be allowed into the geographical area where your facility is located for anywhere from a couple of hours to several weeks.

Identify early those areas of the facility that require priority access. This will expedite damage assessment. If urgent access to certain areas will be required, check with local authorities before anything happens to ascertain the proper procedure. Under special circumstances, they may grant access to qualified individuals.

Emergency Acquisitions

If something goes wrong, what supplies will you need? The contingency plan should include the procedure for acquisitions during emergency, with a list of pre-authorized emergency supplies. Specify by job title who will be responsible for emergency acquisitions, with dollar limits, and procedures to authorize expenditures beyond the limits. Any special accounting requirements should be discussed with the accounting department and incorporated into the contingency plan.

Vital Records

Vital records need to be recovered quickly from off-site backup locations. The contingency plan should specify:

◆ Documents and records likely to be needed first

◆ Where vital records are stored

◆ Equipment and other resources that might be needed for recovery

◆ Where the records will be stored once recovered

Backup Requirements

It's essential to have a backup strategy for hardware, software, data and documentation. The backup strategy should incorporate functions that are critical for the survival of your organization. For example, data files must be backed up regularly and often. All vital records, whether or not computerized, should be protected.

Specify short-term as well as long-term needs. Contingency planning goes beyond simply keeping a backup of records for short-term recovery. In fact, it should be more focused on the long term. In the past, when computer centers tended to be centralized, traditional contingency plans focused on their recovery. With the shift to decentralized information systems, however, contingency planning must now focus on the entire organization, not simply the information processing centers or data centers.

A written backup policy will clarify procedures and prevent operational errors. The policy should specify the backup schedule for each type of data file and how long each generation of data files must be kept.

Recovery from disaster can be expedited if your organization does not use unique hardware or software. Standard technology and up-to-date equipment and software make replacement simple.

Backup Facilities

You need both on-site and off-site backup of hardware, software, data and documentation. On-site backup is convenient and readily accessible; a simple fire-resistant safe may be sufficient. Store in it the most current copy of the backup files.

However, in a disaster, on-site backup tends to be inadequate. Whatever disaster—fire, earthquake, flood (for example, recent hurricanes in Southeast Texas and Louisiana)—affects the primary hardware, software, or data files will also affect the backup. That's why off-site backup storage is necessary.

An off-site facility may be nearby for convenience or far away for enhanced protection. A nearby facility may not be affected by a fire but may be susceptible to damage from natural disasters like earthquakes or hurricanes. For a local off-site facility a fire-resistant safe in a building within a mile or two may provide adequate protection.

A remote off-site facility provides still greater protection. A fire-resistant storage area several miles away may be accessed weekly and used to house data files for a long time. A very remote off-site facility-preferably at least 100 miles away-provides the greatest protection and may be use for archival storage.

Larger organizations will typically keep several generations of backups in different facilities. The logistics of moving files to different facilities can become complex; you'll need procedures to ensure that data files are correctly backed up and transported to the right facilities.

Backup sites may be categorized into three types:

◆ *Hot sites*: Sites that can become fully operational on short notice, typically a few hours. All hardware and software must be compatible with the original site.

◆ *Warm sites*: Sites that can become fully operational in a matter of days or weeks. Less expensive equipment and software may already be in place. More expensive equipment or software is purchased or leased if there is a serious disruption. A partial degradation in processing output is considered acceptable.

◆ *Cold sites*: Sites that have only a skeleton structure in place. It may take anywhere from several days to weeks or even months to get the site operational. Hardware and software are not in place, but there is adequate electrical wiring and air conditioning. A "cold site" has all needed assets in place except the

157

needed computer equipment which is *vendor-dependent* for timely delivery of equipment including the hardware and software.

While hot sites offer considerably faster recovery time, their cost is high. Warm sites are less expensive; cold sites are typically useful for longer-term computing needs. An organization may wish to use all three types of sites in its recovery plan. For example, a hot site could be established for short-term processing needs, giving the company enough time to prepare a warm or cold site for the long run.

For critical applications where a delay in computer processing may cause significant financial loss, you can subscribe to a commercial hot site. Though the cost is high, these sites will guarantee that you'll have properly configured hardware and software to run your data when you really need it.

The costs of commercial hot sites vary considerably. Most vendors charge a monthly subscription fee plus an activation fee and an hourly rate when you actually need to use the site. The activation fee and the hourly rates may be covered by insurance.

Some vendors charge a very high activation fee to discourage use in non-emergency situations. Others encourage their subscribers to use the facilities for non-emergency situations such as overload processing.

Commercial hot sites should not be relied on for an extended period of time. For longer-term needs, there are also commercial warm and cold sites. A warm site subscription typically provides for basic computer facilities with some hardware. The cold site typically provides the infrastructure for a computer facility, such as air conditioning, heating, and humidity controls; wiring for voice and data; electrical wiring; and flood and fire protection. It usually does not contain hardware or software.

In choosing a commercial hot site, consider the number and concentration of subscribers. Too many means that the facility may not be available when needed; too few raises concerns about the financial survival of the business. Look out for a geographic concentration of subscribers: If there's a natural disaster, the site may be unable to meet the needs of all its subscribers.

When you're selecting a hot site, take into account:
- Activation fees
- Monthly fees
- Usage fees
- Contract period and penalty for early termination
- Number of subscribers
- Geographical concentration of subscribers
- Networking capacity
- Customer service and technical assistance
- Hardware and software provided

◆ Ability to upgrade hardware and software if necessary
◆ Vendor's expertise and experience in your industry
◆ Vendor's financial stability
◆ Vendor's experience with actual disasters
◆ References
◆ Other services provided

Mobile backup sites are available from several vendors. These are trailers equipped with computer hardware and software that can be taken to any location you desire. This setup is especially helpful where it may be difficult for the personnel to commute to a remote backup facility.

To identify the best recovery strategy you'll need to conduct a thorough technical as well as cost-benefit analysis. Don't forget how much it costs for wiring, air conditioning, and fire prevention.

Mutual Aid Agreements

Mutual aid agreements are a low-cost alternative for emergency processing: Two or more organizations with similar equipment and applications promise to help each other in an emergency. These agreements may not be legally enforceable so they shouldn't be relied on exclusively, but they make sense especially for companies with special requirements that may be unable to use commercial hot sites.

If you're thinking about a mutual aid agreement, ask yourself:

◆ What are the differences in equipment between my company and the potential partner?
◆ What are the differences in applications?
◆ How will we maintain compatibility in equipment and software with the partner over time?
◆ How often will we test our systems for compatibility?
◆ In an emergency, how much processing time will they have available? If there are multiple partners, which one will we use?
◆ What equipment, software, staff assistance, and facilities will the partner provide?
◆ How secure are the potential partner's computer facilities?

Relocating Facilities

The severity of the damage to your own facilities will dictate whether your organization relocates temporarily or permanently. The contingency plan should cover both possibilities. Recovering from a disaster may take a long time; but what happens in the interim? For example, if only a portion of your facilities can be used:

◆ Which departments or functions will go back in first?

◆ What type of support will they require?

◆ Can large departments be split up, operating out of two or more locations?

Factors to think about with regard to relocating include:

◆ Square footage needed

◆ Which departments need to be in proximity

◆ Communications facilities needed

◆ Security concerns

◆ Storage area needed

◆ Access to public transportation

◆ Parking needed

◆ Employee requirements, such as housing, schools, day care, etc. (if relocating at a distance)

Hardware Backup

Many organizations think that hardware backup is all that's needed for contingency planning, but hardware backup alone is not sufficient for most companies. While hardware is an essential element of contingency planning, there's a lot more to it.

It *is* important to have backup hardware available both on and off-site. For smaller disruptions, only one or at most a few pieces of equipment are likely to be affected. On-site backup is usually sufficient to resolve such problems. To save on costs you might consider using older or slower systems in emergencies. Sometimes partial processing capability is acceptable.

For more serious disruptions, which tend to be longer, off-site hardware is of considerable importance. While hardware vendors are naturally the best source for replacement equipment, the vendor may be unable to supply the equipment you need quickly enough for you. If that's so, used hardware dealers may be able to supply critical components on short notice.

Software and Data Backup

Software and data are intangible assets that must be protected. Software includes the operating system, utilities, and application programs. Keep backup copies not only of your primary software but also of any upgrades or patches to fix bugs, and of user manuals (online or hard copy). It's unnecessary to keep backup copies of older generation software.

You need backup copies of the software and user manuals at both primary and off-site facilities, where you also need copies of the software configuration files or other special settings. Don't forget to upgrade software at both facilities at the same time, and set in place a procedure to ensure that copies of maintenance patches to the software are also kept off-site. Check the legal requirements for making backups. Some vendors require an additional licensing fee if the software will be used in an alternate facility.

Data includes all source documents, electronic data files and databases, and output documents. Unlike software, data by its very nature changes continuously. The contingency plan should prepare for rapid recovery of data.

There are several different techniques for backing up data. For small files the process may be as simple as making a duplicate on the backup medium. When it's either not practical or not cost-effective to backup the entire file, try something else.

In a batch processing system, a new master file is created using the old master and updating it with transactional changes. Keeping copies of the old master file for two or three generations, along with copies of the transaction file updates, provides for continuous backup of the data.

A real-time online processing system requires different procedures. Duplicate logging of transactions may be necessary. Copies of individual records may have to be kept before updating. Other techniques, such as before-and-after images of master records, may be useful. Specialized backup procedures are typically an integral part of database management systems.

Before recovering data from backup files, it's advisable always to duplicate the backup file to prevent accidents. Data integrity during the reconstruction process can then be ensured with special supervision and controls.

Documentation Backup

Along with hardware, software, and data, backup user manuals and other documentation should be stored in an off-site fire-resistant location. When changes are made to the primary manuals and documentation, make sure that the backup documentation is updated as well.

Systems and program documentation that should be backed up include:

◆ Source code for programs
◆ Flowcharts
◆ Program logic descriptions
◆ Error conditions

Vital Records and Source Documents

While most organizations store backup copies of vital records off-site, there are still numerous documents that may only be in the primary facilities because they have not yet been backed up. Many of these are source documents like invoices or purchase orders that originate outside the organization. If a source document is critical and the information in it cannot be easily reconstructed if the document is destroyed, you need a procedure to copy the source document.

Remote Backup

Several companies offer remote backup using the Internet. Periodically, usually once a day, your data files can be automatically backed up to an off-site computer facility where the data is stored in an encrypted form. Companies that offer remote backup include:

- ◆ Atrieva: http://www.atrieva.com/
- ◆ Connected Corporation: http://www.connected.com./
- ◆ Guardian Computer Service: http://www.guardiancomputer.com/
- ◆ Netsafe: http://www.evault.com/
- ◆ Saf-T-Net: http://www.trgcomm.com/
- ◆ SafeGuard Interactive: http://www.sgii.com/
- ◆ TeleBackup Systems, Inc.: http://www.telebackup.com/

A more costly alternative is to transmit a copy of each transaction to a remote facility.

In *mirror processing* the data is not only transmitted but also updated on a duplicate database. With mirror processing the backup database is always current. This doesn't necessarily have to be done at a remote location; you may want to set it up on-site.

Fire Safety

Fire is the most common cause of damage to computer centers. Combustible material should not be allowed in any computer room. Install fire-detectors in vulnerable locations. Use fire-retardant material for office furniture, draperies, and any floor coverings. Put waste receptacles outside the computer room: Computer paper in waste receptacles can accelerate a fire.

Detection Devices

Fire detectors sense either thermal combustion and its byproducts or changes in temperature. They may be actuated by smoke, heat, or flame. All detectors must meet government standards. Make sure the devices are connected to an automatic fire alarm system.

Smoke-actuated devices provide early warning of fires developing slowly. They should be installed in all air conditioning and ventilating systems. Smoke detectors typically rely on either *photoelectric* or *radioactive* devices.

In the photoelectric cell, variations in the intensity of light cause changes in electric current. These detectors are generally of three types:

◆ *Area-sampling* devices draw in air from the area to be protected. If smoke is present in the sampled air, the light reflections on the photoelectric cell will trigger the alarm.

◆ *Beam* devices focus a beam of light onto a photoelectric cell from across the protected area. Smoke, causing an obstruction in the light, activates the alarm.

◆ *Spot* devices, unlike beam devices, contain the light source and the receiver in one unit. Smoke entering the detector causes the light to reflect onto the photoelectric cell, activating the alarm.

Radioactive smoke detectors contain a minute amount of radioactive material in a special housing (the danger from radiation from such devices is minimal). Smoke interacting with the radioactive material changes its ionization, which activates the alarm. Radioactive detectors are mostly commonly *spot* types.

The response time for radioactive smoke detectors is affected by several variables, including the stratification of air currents and the nature of the combustion products. Generally, the heavier the particles resulting from combustion, the longer it takes for them to reach the ceiling, where the smoke detectors are usually attached, and the longer the response time of the unit.

Heat-actuated detectors can be of two types. The first will activate the alarm when the temperature reaches a predetermined value. The second senses the amount of change in temperature. Typically, when the rise in temperature exceeds 15 degrees to 20 degrees F the alarm is activated.

In highly combustible areas, the rate-of-rise temperature detectors are recommended because their response time is faster. However, fixed temperature detectors are not as prone to false alarms. Some heat-actuated detectors contain both types of sensors.

Heat detectors are available in line or spot styles. *Line-type detectors* usually rely on heat-sensitive cables or a pneumatic tube. *Spot-type detectors* are placed at fixed intervals in each zone.

Flame-actuated detectors are of two types, both expensive: flame-radiation-frequency and flame-energy. *Flame-radiation-frequency* detectors sense the flame-related flicker caused by combustion. Flame-energy detectors sense the infrared energy of the flame. They tend to be best-suited to protecting expensive equipment; their

163

principle advantage is that they are super-fast. These detectors can also produce enough voltage to trigger the release of an extinguishing agent.

Extinguishing Agents

Different types of fire require different types of extinguishing agents. Using the wrong extinguishing agent can do more harm than good.

◆ Fires fed by *ordinary combustible materials*, such as wood, paper, plastics, and fabric, can be safely extinguished with water or triclass (ABC) dry chemical.

◆ Fires fed by *flammable liquids and gases*, such as oil, grease, gasoline, or paint can generally be safely extinguished with tri-class (ABC) dry chemical, halon, FM-200, and carbon dioxide.

◆ Fires involving *live electrical equipment* should be extinguished only with a non-conducting agent such as tri-class (ABC), regular dry chemical, halon, or carbon dioxide.

Hand-held fire extinguishers should be mounted on the wall, as should self-contained breathing apparatus, because carbon dioxide discharge can suffocate humans.

Electrical Fires

Most computer room fires will be electrical, caused by overheating of wire insulation or other components. Because smoke from an electrical fire may be toxic, it should be avoided even in small quantities. Generally electrical fires cannot be extinguished until the heat source is eliminated.

A power panel with circuit breakers for the major pieces of equipment should be easily accessible, preferably inside the computer room. The circuits should be clearly labeled so that equipment can be shut down quickly in an emergency. There should be separate circuits for redundant devices, and an emergency switch to shut down everything if there is a fire.

In a major fire or explosion, the only concern should be the safety of human life. Computer equipment and wiring is likely to be destroyed by the intense heat. That's why backup copies of disks and data should always be kept off-site. Not only will this help in recovering from a fire, it can also help during the fire since the staff will not be tempted to risk their lives saving data.

Carbon dioxide, a colorless, odorless, and electrically non-conductive inert gas, is generally stored under pressure as a liquid. Carbon dioxide extinguishes fire by reducing the amount of oxygen available to it. It may not be effective on fires fed by materials such as metal hydrides, reactive metals like sodium, potassium, magnesium, titanium, and zirconium, and chemicals containing oxygen available for combustion.

Halon has the potential of depleting the ozone layer. While halon is still in use, by international agreement it has not been manufactured since January 1, 1994. FM-200, a substitute, is not very effective against electrical fires. In an electrical fire, it's essential that the power be shut off because until power is stopped a fire extinguishing system will only suppress, not extinguish, the fire.

The suppression agent in FM-200 is a halogenated alkane, heptafluoropropane. Under compression FM-200, a colorless and odorless gas, becomes a liquid, which is stored in steel cylinders.

Once discharged, FM-200 returns to the gaseous state. It suppresses fire by cooling it and reducing the amount of oxygen available. It's typically discharged rapidly, in no more than a few seconds. FM-200 helps prevent re-ignition. It doesn't have any residue nor does it require cleanup after discharge and it doesn't harm humans.

Water Sprinklers

Water sprinkler systems are a simple, relatively inexpensive protection against fire. Most new buildings are required by code to have sprinkler systems, though their accidental activation can cause substantial damage and it may take a long time before normal operations can be resumed.

In an electrical fire, water may even intensify the fire, causing greater damage. Sensors should therefore be installed to cut off electrical power before sprinklers are turned on. It should also be possible to activate sprinkler heads individually to prevent damage to a wide area. A shut-off valve inside the computer room can help you shut off water when it's no longer needed, minimizing damage if the system is accidentally activated.

Carbon dioxide, halon, and FM-200 extinguishers don't require any cleanup after discharge. Foam or dry chemicals can be hard to remove. Quick removal of smoke should be a priority. The smoke or fire alarm should automatically activate special fans and blowers.

Extinguishing Micro-computer Fires

If computer equipment starts smoking, first cut off the equipment's electrical power. This is often sufficient to extinguish the fire by itself. If there are visible signs of fire, or if you can feel the heat, use a fire extinguisher. Carbon dioxide extinguishers are often recommended for microcomputer-related fires. When using a carbon dioxide extinguisher, don't spray the agent directly onto the surface of the CRT (cathode-ray tube) because the sudden drop in temperature it causes will shatter the glass.

Training

Personnel should be trained for a fire emergency. Company policy should state exactly what action should be taken if a fire starts or a smoke alarm goes off. Personnel should be strictly prohibited from risking injury or loss of life to protect data or equipment.

Preventing Damage

The following steps can reduce the damage caused by fire, and in the process reduce your insurance premiums:

◆ Safes for storage of documents should have a minimum four-hour fire rating.

◆ Walls, floors, and ceilings of computer facilities should have a minimum two-hour fire rating.

◆ The fire alarm should ring simultaneously at the computer facility and the nearest fire station. In addition, fire alarm signals should be located to assure prompt response.

◆ Vaults storing backup tapes and records should be in a separate building at a sufficient distance.

◆ Smoke and ionization detection system should be installed on the ceiling of the computer facilities. Water detection systems should be installed under the floors.

◆ Halon, FM-200, or a similar chemical extinguishing system should be installed throughout the facilities. Automatic sprinkler systems can be used in supply and support areas.

◆ Building code and fire marshal regulations must be adhered to strictly.

Fire Tracer and Win Tracer

Fire Tracer products (http://www.emss.net) give the exact location of the source of a developing fire in a computer cabinet, control equipment set, or room. They can also be used for air handling units, return air grills, ducts, and large open areas, supported by air sampling techniques. With these products, air is pumped into a series of micro-bore tubes positioned in a cabinet, room, or compartment being protected. The sample of air is then analyzed for the presence of either smoke particles or gas. If the smoke level reaches a preset trace level, then the Fire Tracer switches from a sampling mode to a search mode to identify the exact location of the smoke source.

Three separate alarms are triggered by the system. The first alarm level is triggered when the trace cycle is initiated. A pre-alarm is triggered to warn that a potential fire exists in the identified area. The final alarm indicates that a full incipient fire condition is present. Each of the three alarms may be connected to a fire panel for control purposes.

WinTracer control software may be used to monitor and control FireTracers. WinTracer provides:

◆ Warning when smoke levels exceed preset limits

◆ Location of the alarm

◆ Action sequences and hazard indications

◆ Remote control (reset, off/online & changing functions, such as alarm levels, etc.)

◆ Display of site statues (tracers which are on/offline, etc.)

◆ Historical trends

◆ Data logging and recording of significant events

The basic display is simple enough to be monitored by an unskilled operator. Bar graphs display current levels of smoke or gas. Color-coding indicates when current levels exceed the alert levels. If there is an alarm, there is a text description of the alarm source, supplemented by a site map pinpointing the location, along with actions to be taken for different alarm types and locations (e.g., notes to tell operator to phone fire station, clear room, whatever) and a list of hazards near the alarm locations.

WinTracer can be customized and the data analyzed. The administration has remote programming access to change text descriptions, actions sequences, and hazard lists. Alarms may be acknowledged or cancelled. Trend graphs can be plotted to monitor compliance.

Insurance

Your insurance, with the right endorsements, must be adequate to protect against disruptions in business. Your contingency plan should address insurance concerns both before and after a disaster. Especially be sure you're covered if access to the facilities is delayed.

Standard insurance policies treat computer equipment like industrial equipment, covering them for the same threats. Standard policies don't cover computer equipment for power outages or electrostatic discharges that may delete or destroy electronically stored information.

A policy specifically geared toward electronic data processing (EDP) typically covers risks to computers, including replacement or repair. For all high-technology assets, the policy should contain a *replacement cost* endorsement. Unlike assets like industrial machinery with a long life and low depreciation rate, computer equipment tends to depreciate rapidly, losing its value. Without the replacement cost endorsement, you may not be able to afford to replace computer equipment after a disaster.

EDP policies, however, typically don't cover damages resulting from loss or inability to access computer equipment. That's why you need business interruption and out-of-pocket expenses insurance. *Business Interruption* insurance covers not only losses caused directly by the disaster, but also future business losses if operations can't resume quickly. *Out-of-pocket expense* coverage reimburses you for use of alternate computer facilities. Make sure your operations at the outsourcing vendor's facilities are covered.

Keep your insurance policies up to date. Many organizations just keep on renewing a policy they bought years ago, though the business environment is continuously changing. A policy that provided adequate coverage even three years ago may fall short for current needs.

Maintain a running list of organizational assets, along with their appraised values, updating it every time an asset is added or retired. Certainly review it at least once or twice a year, and, of course, store a copy of the list off-site.

Many insurance policies require policyholders to insure their property to 80%, 90%, or 100% of its value, penalizing them if they fail to maintain the proper level. To reduce your chances of being penalized, have your assets appraised periodically and insured to the value required by the policy.

Check that your *valuable papers and records'* coverage includes the cost of recreating documents, such as re-entering data and restoring damaged items.

Software products are often excluded from insurance policies unless there is a specific endorsement, but you need to have them covered in case there's a breakdown in equipment, such as a system crash.

Conclusion

Many organizations have no workable disaster recovery plan. A common mistake is to put too much emphasis on electronic data processing and computer recovery and too little on keeping the business running. Many business functions may be able to survive with manual procedures. Prepare procedures to support the essential functions of your business until computer processing is re-established.

Both user participation and the support of senior management are critical in formulating an effective contingency plan. Preventive controls in a system anticipate and avoid deviations. Examples include training of personnel, segregation of duties, prenumbered forms, documentation, passwords, compatibility tests, and turnaround documents. Preventive controls are usually more cost beneficial as compared with other controls because they avoid the costs of deviations and the costs of correction.

Many contingency plans provide unnecessary details and lack flexibility. Too much information makes it difficult to update and revise the plan. Anything that can be dealt with at the time of the disaster should be left out, as should anything that cannot be determined until the effect of a disaster has been evaluated.

Contingency plans should be reviewed, tested, and updated at least annually. At each review ask yourself:

◆ What does the organization need now and in the future to survive after a disaster?

◆ How are these needs likely to be fulfilled by the strategies selected in the plan?

◆ How can the strategies be made more effective?

Those who were responsible for developing the contingency plan should not review, test, or evaluate it. Independent individuals will have greater objectivity and insight.

Disasters and catastrophes are extremely rare. It's therefore imperative that your contingency plan be cost-effective, though the cost-benefit analysis is admittedly very difficult for rare events. Furthermore, your company's risk preference will affect how much risk you can tolerate.

Senior managers are ultimately responsible for contingency planning. While they may delegate many details to middle management and staff, they must play an integral part in the creation of the plan.

Chapter 9
Auditing and Legal Issues

Most organizations are facing a host of technologies ranging from e-commerce, the Internet, the Intranet, data mining, data analysis, data warehousing, electronic bulletin board systems (BBS), telecommunications to enterprise-wide applications, artificial intelligence expert systems, neural networks, and client-server computing. All business processes today depend on effective and efficient information processing. For example, electronic bulletin board systems function as a centralized information source and message switching system for a particular interest group. Users review and leave messages for other users, and communicate with other users on the system at the same time. Auditors may use computers in many ways to simplify and enhance the audit process. The auditor can work independently of the auditee and can access records at remote sites without travel.

Laws and public policies to regulate the use of these technologies have not kept pace with their development. For example, legal boundaries to protect confidentiality and integrity of data are of concern to security professionals.

The two requirements crucial to achieving audit efficiency and effectiveness with a personal computer are selecting the appropriate audit tasks for personal computer applications and the appropriate software to perform the selected audit tasks.

The auditor has an ever-increasing number of roles to play in computer environments. These include:

◆ Evaluating management's computer system controls in the course of an audit.
◆ Using the computer as a tool to perform the audit more efficiently and effectively.

Security Auditing

The field of security auditing may be broadly classified into two types, internal and external. Both rely on the independent appraisal function; however, their scope is different.

Internal auditors typically work for a given organization. External auditors do not. They are typically Certified Public Accountants (CPAs) or Chartered Accountants (CAs) hired to perform an independent audit, usually of a company's financial statements. Their primary concern is to evaluate the fairness of the statements.

The scope of internal auditing is typically broader. Internal auditors are concerned not only with safeguarding organizational assets but also with promoting operational efficiency. Their concern is that the company has adequate controls and that the procedures used are cost-efficient as well as effective. Internal auditors typically report to top management or to the audit committee of the Board of Directors.

The information technology (IT) function can be audited by both internal and external auditors. Whoever does it must have expertise in both financial auditing and computer technology. IT auditors can help your company assess the risks related to the use of computer technology.

Coordinating the activities of IT auditors and financial auditors can enhance audit efficiency. IT auditors might train and guide non-IT auditors in IT procedures and methods; or IT auditors might manage the computer system during financial audit processing.

IT auditors recommend appropriate controls, which tend to be more complex than controls in manual systems. Specialized computer audit techniques must be used in highly automated environments. IT auditing:

◆ Uses technological tools and expertise

◆ Evaluates the adequacy and effectiveness of the control systems

◆ Assesses technology-related risks

IT auditors review systems to ensure that they meet quality criteria, assessing their compliance with the organization's systems development methodology. IT auditors may review proposed enhancements to computer systems to evaluate whether the system contains adequate controls. Their participation in the development process avoids the need to modify systems after they've been implemented, a costly and difficult process. It may, in fact, sometimes be virtually impossible to correctly modify a system. An auditor should review trading partner agreements and contracts with third-party service providers. These documents should contain necessary clauses and appropriately limit liabilities. Moreover, legal counsel should have reviewed the agreements or contracts. An auditor should also determine whether the third-party service provider's operations and controls have been independently reviewed (for example, by public accountants).

While IT auditors may evaluate systems in process, the IT auditor must not assume any operational responsibility. The auditors must remain independent and objective.

Data centers serve the information needs of an organization. IT auditors typically review the following aspects of the data center:

- Systems development standards
- Efficiency and effectiveness of operating and administrative procedures
- Library control procedures
- Structure of the data center
- Network system
- Backup controls
- Contingency planning and disaster recovery
- Personnel practices
- Security

To perform their duties IT auditors must:

- Keep current with state-of-the-art technologies
- Understand how to use the technology to support business functions
- Use audit tools specific to the technology needs of the organization

IT auditors often review applications systems, with special attention to programmed control procedures such as edit checks and exception reporting. Among their duties, IT auditors:

- Evaluate the risks and control associated with technology
- Support other auditing functions during financial, operations, or compliance audits
- Evaluate corporate computer policy and security standards

The IT auditor is also responsible for determining whether controls are adequate and whether:

- Transactions are processed accurately and completely
- Transactions are properly authorized
- Errors and omissions are prevented or detected
- Duties are segregated
- Jobs are completed in a timely fashion

IT auditors often assist external and operational internal auditors in:

- Collecting, extracting, and analyzing data
- Reviewing and testing internal controls
- Investigating exceptions

173

Audit Trail

E-business systems should be periodically examined, or audited, by a company's internal auditing staff or external auditors from professional accounting firms. Such audits should review and evaluate whether proper and adequate security measures and management policies have been developed and implemented. An important objective of e-business system audits is testing the integrity of an application audit trail. An *audit trail* can be defined as the presence of documentation that allows a transaction to be traced through all stages of its information processing. The audit trail of manual information systems was quite visible and easy to trace; however, computer-based information systems have changed the form of the audit trail.

The transaction trail or audit trail allows the auditor to trace a transaction back to its origins. All attempts to gain access to the system should be logged chronologically. Unusual activity and variations from established procedures should be identified and investigated.

Many significant transactions occur inside the computer, so they aren't visible or directly observable. The transaction trail provided information about additions, deletions, or modifications to data within the system. An effective audit trail allows the data to be retrieved and certified. Audit trails will give information such as:

◆ Date and time of the transaction

◆ Who processed the transaction

◆ At which terminal the transaction was processed

Maintaining audit trails is more difficult in an electronic environment. In a paper based system, for instance, a physical purchase order is prepared, typically in triplicate. At each state, paper is work done and a physical trail established. Such a trail is normally absent in electronic transactions.

Your computer software should be designed to provide an audit trail. Most commercial software packages have at least some audit trail capability.

Computer security risks affect an organization's internal control structure, which in turn affects the ability to audit the entity. Computer processing reduces human involvement, centralizes data, and may eliminate segregation of duties. Centralizing data makes it possible to introduce higher quality controls over operations; however, due to reduced human involvement and less segregation of duties, auditors must use great care in evaluating the electronic data processing department.

Adequate segregation of duties is crucial. No person should be in a position both to perpetrate and to conceal errors in the normal course of business. For example, there should be a division of duties between:

◆ Programmers, librarians, and operators: Different individuals should develop computer applications, have custody of programs and data files, and operate applications.

◆ Data processing personnel, users, and control personnel

◆ Individuals authorizing changes in program logic or data and those coding the changes

EDI and Electronic Contracting

Electronic data interchange (EDI) systems are on-line systems where computers automatically perform transactions such as order processing and generating invoices. EDI allows trading partners to exchange electronic data faster, cheaper, and more accurately. The messages are structured in a prearranged format to facilitate automatic computer processing. The electronic messages generally result in a legally binding contract.

Although EDI can reduce costs, it can adversely affect an auditor's ability to do her job. EDI transactions go through several systems. Electronic records and audit trail must be maintained throughout. Any data used for EDI needs to be translated into a standardized format. The translation software must maintain the audit trail. Any communication sent over the network must be accounted for by communication software. Data translated into internal format by the recipient's translation software must be tracked. Finally, the data is used by the recipient's application software.

In an EDI environment, a weakness in any system can create problems not just for that entity but also for its trading partners. Therefore, each function at each stage must be reviewed and appropriate controls incorporated.

The American Institute of Certified Public Accountants (AICPA) has issued control techniques to ensure the integrity of an EDI system. The AICPA recommends that controls over accuracy and completeness at the application level include:

◆ Checks on performance to determine compliance with industry standards

◆ Checks on sequence numbering for transactions

◆ Prompt reporting of irregularities

◆ Verification of adequacy of audit trails

◆ Checks of embedded headers and trailers at interchange, functional group, and transaction set level

Control techniques at the environmental level include:

◆ Quality assurance review of vendor software

◆ Segregation of duties

◆ Ensuring that software is virus-free

◆ Procuring an audit report from the vendor's auditors

◆ Evidence of testing

To ensure that all EDI transactions are authorized, the AICPA suggests these controls include:

◆ Operator identification code
◆ Operator profile
◆ Trading partner identifier
◆ Maintenance of user access variables
◆ Regular changing of passwords

Not all electronic messages result in electronic contracting. For example, messages with purely informational content don't nor do intrafirm messages; the law generally distinguishes between intra-firm and inter-firm communications.

Yet electronic contracting occurs routinely. Examples of electronic offer and acceptance modes are:

◆ Purchase orders
◆ Invoices
◆ Payments
◆ Solicitation and submission of bids
◆ Filing documents with the government
◆ Advertising goods and services

Trading partner agreements or EDI agreements are essential to electronic contracting. These agreements:

◆ Clarify each party's rights and obligations
◆ Specify the risk and liability of each party
◆ Help avoid misunderstandings

A trading partner agreement gives the parties the legal right to enforce it. These agreements affect partners only; they don't cover third parties, such as VANs. The legal and EDI communities (e.g., the American Bar Association and the EDI Council of Canada) have drafted several model trading partner agreements. There are also model agreements for specific industries and countries. Though the models provide a fair and balanced contract, most businesses will want to customize them to their own needs.

A trading partner agreement should state the intent of the parties to transact business electronically. It should specify whether all trade or only a specified portion of the trade between the two parties is covered by the agreement. It should clearly specify which transaction sets will constitute a legally enforceable offer and acceptance and how electronic payments will be made. The parties should acknowledge that they will not repudiate the validity, integrity, or reliability of EDI transactions and will consider them the equivalent of paper-based transactions.

The parties must agree on the time and place of recipient of EDI communications.

There are several possibilities. Receipt may take place when:

◆ A message is sent by the sender's computer system

◆ A message is received by the receiver's computer system

◆ A message is received at the receiver's mailbox on a VAN or other third party computer system

◆ An acknowledgement of receipt is sent by the recipient

◆ An acknowledgement of receipt is received by the sender

Acknowledgements, typically used to verify communications, provide proof of a transaction's integrity and authority. Use cryptographic methods whenever possible, especially when the authenticity of a transaction is crucial. Sometimes electronic signatures are used to verify the integrity of a message; typically these signatures are created cryptographically; however, a signature doesn't have to be encrypted. Any symbol or party's name may be considered sufficient as a signature for purposes of offer and acceptance as long as the EDI system is trustworthy. The location of the signature in messages should be agreed on in advance and be as uniform as possible.

Security considerations need special attention when you're drafting a trading partners' agreement. Security provides confidence that transactions are authentic. It's needed to ensure that the transactions remain confidential. The EDI system's security is essential in determining whether electronic contracting is legally enforceable.

From a legal perspective, trading partner agreements generally require commercially reasonable security, but the definition of commercially reasonable is vague, differing from industry to industry. For example, banking will require a much higher level of security than on-line retailing of software.

The trading partner agreement should discuss the security responsibilities of each party. For instance, to what extent is one party responsible for ensuring the security of its trading partner? What actions will be taken if security is breached? Basic EDI security risks include:

◆ Access violations

◆ Message modifications

◆ Interruptions or delays

◆ Message rerouting

◆ Message repudiation

Without access controls, an unauthorized individual could initiate a transaction by pretending to be an authorized trading partner. Fictitious purchase orders may be sent or fictitious payments made. The reliability and integrity of the EDI system break down without appropriate access controls. Greater security is achieved by combining several access control techniques. Most common are techniques based on:

- Something a person knows, such as a password
- Something a person possesses, such as a magnetic card or a token
- Some unique attribute of a person, such as a fingerprint, a voice print, or a retinal pattern

Unauthorized individuals may intentionally modify electronic messages. Messages may also be modified unintentionally through hardware, software, or transmission error. Authentication of messages is a major concern, especially with respect to repudiation of a transaction. Irrevocable proof, such as a digital signature, minimizes the risk of repudiation.

Auditing Contingency Plans

Data processing serves the information needs of most organizations and its survival in a disaster is often critical. Auditors are therefore especially concerned about the viability of the disaster recovery plan.

Your contingency plan is a valuable document that needs to be audited like any other asset. An auditor is responsible for investigating, evaluating, and verifying controls, which may reduce the risks associated with various types of disasters.

Avoiding disaster is always preferable to recovering from disaster. An effective contingency plan, audited regularly, can sometimes help prevent a disaster. For example, sabotage can be prevented, but when it isn't, saboteurs can often hide their activities. Auditing may help detect the crime.

Controls

Management is responsible for installing and maintaining controls, which are used to reduce the probability of attack on computer security. The auditor is responsible for determining whether the controls are adequate and whether they are being complied with. As more controls are incorporated, the operating costs tend to increase. Some types of controls are discussed below.

Deterrent controls are used to encourage compliance with controls. Deterrents are relatively inexpensive to implement. Since their purpose is to deter crime, however, it's often difficult to measure their effectiveness. Deterrent controls are meant to complement other controls; they're not sufficient by themselves.

Preventive controls are the first line of defense. Their purpose is to thwart perpetrators trying to gain access to your system. They also help prevent unintentional errors from affecting the system and the data. For example, pre-numbered documents ensure that there isn't a failure in recording a transaction. Data validation and review procedures prevent the recording of an incorrect or incomplete transaction, or duplicates of a transaction.

Detective controls help detect an error once a system has been violated. These controls prevent the error from harming the system. Their purpose is to focus attention on the problem. For example, a bait file will identify unauthorized use such as when a dummy (non-existent) record is processed, or there may be a comparison between standard run time and actual run time to spot possible misuse.

Corrective controls reduce the impact of the threat after a loss has occurred. They aid in recovering from damage or in reducing the effect of damage. Corrective controls may provide data for recovery procedures. For instance, lost information on floppies may be restored with utility programs.

Application controls are built into software to deter or detect irregularities and minimize errors. Application controls typically include input, processing, change, testing, output, and procedural controls.

- ◆ Input controls are used to ensure that transactions are authorized, processed correctly, and processed only once. Input controls may reject, correct, or resubmit data.
- ◆ Processing controls ensure that transactions entered into the system are valid and accurate, that external data is not lost or altered, and that invalid transactions are reprocessed correctly.
- ◆ Change controls safeguard the integrity of the system. Standards are established for making modifications. All changes must be documented.
- ◆ Test controls ensure that a system is reliable before it becomes operational. An example would be the processing of limited test data when using the new system.
- ◆ Output controls authenticate other controls. They verify that authorized transactions are processed correctly. Random comparisons can be made of output to input to verify correct processing.
- ◆ Procedural controls help reduce the probability of processing mistakes and assure continued functioning if a failure does occur.

Audit Software

Computer-assisted audit techniques are used extensively; large quantities of electronically stored data can be tested quickly and accurately using audit software. Query languages can create ad hoc reports and perform a variety of audit procedures. Audit software functions typically:

- ◆ Appraise reasonableness (e.g., accuracy of sales discounts) and trends, including aging analysis
- ◆ Check for duplicate invoices or payments
- ◆ Compare financial data on different files for consistency
- ◆ Analyze and report data

- Extract data from computer files
- Provide exception reporting (e.g., excessive inventory balances or an unusual employee salary)
- Do field comparisons to find errors or inconsistencies
- Detect fraud
- Recalculate balances
- Do statistical sampling and analysis

Generalized audit software can identify errors keyed into accounting software. It provides cost savings over custom software because most audits involve similar activities, such as:

- Analyzing data for unusual or erroneous values
- Analyzing or comparing data stored in two or more separate but logically related files
- Generating and formatting reports
- Recalculating balances
- Selecting a sample
- Stratifying data
- Testing transactions

An example of popular generalized audit software packages is ACL Software (888.669.4225 or www.acl.com).

You can customize audit software if the generalized variety doesn't fulfill the needs of your organization. Specialized audit software is in any case available for specific industries, such as banking, health care, entertainment, or insurance.

Legal Liability in Security Management

Computer security law is a relatively new field, and the legal establishment has yet to reach a consensus on a host of important issues. Nonetheless, you can incur substantial legal liability by not maintaining adequate security. Management may be held personally liable in certain instances. Be particularly careful to protect privacy and other personal rights, which are easily violated due to a lack of computer security.

Legislation

The Financial Privacy Act of 1978 was passed to protect information. The 1987 Computer Security Act further protects privacy and increases government computer security requirements. This act states that " improving the security and privacy of sensitive information in the federal computer systems is in the public interest." The private sector also has to ensure that confidential information is kept private.

The 1987 Computer Security Act gave the National Institute of Standards and Technology (NIST) responsibility to develop cost-effective standards to protect confidential information in federal databases. Private companies can use NIST's work as a model for their own standards.

Once information is determined to be sensitive, it should be verified for accuracy before being put into a database and given whatever protection is necessary to keep it confidential. Ask yourself the following questions:

◆ How should this information be classified?

◆ How can we ensure the accuracy of the information?

◆ How can we protect sensitive or confidential information?

The Computer Fraud and Abuse Act of 1986 makes any unauthorized use (copying, damaging, obtaining database information, etc.) of computer hardware or software across state lines a crime.

The Foreign Corrupt Practices Act of 1977 applies to companies whose securities are registered or filed under the Securities Exchange Act of 1934. It requires these companies to keep accurate accounting records and to maintain a system of internal control.

The Counterfeit Access Device and Computer Fraud and Abuse Act of 1984 covers unauthorized retrieval of data from the computer files of a financial institution or a credit reporting agency.

The Electronic Communications Privacy Act of 1986 prohibits anyone from intercepting information being transmitted electronically.

Negligence and Due Care

You can incur liability for security violations in a variety of situations, ranging from programming errors to violations of civil or criminal law.

The standard to avoid liability is due care. For instance, you may have properly designed and coded a computer program but, because security is inadequate, a saboteur places a logic bomb that causes the program to crash. The organization and its senior managers may be held personally liable for any damages arising from the crash if negligence in securing the program can be proved. Such damages may be significant if, for example, they cause a loss in market price of the stock or, worse, if human life is affected, as in the crash of a medical diagnosis system.

NIST has published several national standards for computer security. They cover:

◆ Automated password generators

◆ Contingency planning

◆ Data encryption

◆ Digital signatures

◆ Electrical power for computer facilities

◆ Key management

◆ Password usage

◆ Physical security and risk management

◆ User authentication techniques

The Department of Defense (DOD) publishes the Rainbow Series of booklets to help developers, evaluators, and users of trusted systems. They include information on networks, databases, and other problems with distributed computer systems. The governments of Britain, the Netherlands, France, and Germany have themselves jointly issued detailed Information Technology Security Evaluation Criteria (ITSEC).

Consider using these standards in managing your own computer security. If you don't, in a lawsuit alleging breach of security, the plaintiff may use your failure to follow recognized standards to prove that you've been negligent, even if your organization wasn't required to follow them.

Chapter 10
Computer Crime, Cyberfraud and Recent Trends

Computer crime is a growing threat to society by the criminal or irresponsible actions of computer individuals who are taking advantage of the widespread use and vulnerability of computers and the Internet and other networks. It thus presents a major challenge to the ethical use of information technologies. E-computer crime poses serious threats to the integrity, safety, and survival of most e-business systems, and thus makes the development of effective security methods a top priority.

Computer Crime

Computer crime is defined by the Association of Information Technology professionals (ATIP) as including:

- The unauthorized use, access, modification, and destruction of hardware, software, data, or network resources.
- The unauthorized release of information
- The unauthorized copying of software
- Denying an end user access to his or her own hardware, software, data, or network resources
- Using or conspiring to use computer or network resources to illegally obtain information or tangible property.

Penalties for violation of the U.S. Computer Fraud and Abuse Act include:

1. 1 to 5 years in prison for a first offence
2. 10 years for a second offence

3.   20 years for three or more offences

4.   Fines ranging up to $250,000 or twice the value of stolen data

Hacking

Hacking is the obsessive use of computers, or the unauthorized access and use of networked computer systems. Illegal hackers (also called *crackers*) frequently assault the Internet and other networks to steal or damage data and programs. Hackers can:

◆ Monitor e-mail, Web server access, or file transfers to extract passwords or steal network files, or to plant data that will cause a system to welcome intruders.

◆ Use remote services that allow one computer on a network to execute programs on another computer to gain privileged access within a network.

◆ Use Telnet, an Internet tool for interactive use of remote computers, to discover information to plan other attacks.

Note: The more likely danger by far is the cleaning crew that's been bribed to snatch diskettes off your desk, the disgruntled employee who knows the passwords and the encryption keys, the bookkeeper who's created a fake vendor account, the wag who's pulling racist jokes off the web and e-mailing them to half the company. These insiders might not qualify as computer criminals, but computers can certainly facilitate their dirty deeds.

Cyber-Theft

Many computer crimes involve the theft of money. In the majority of cases, they are "inside jobs" that involve unauthorized network entry and fraudulent alteration of computer databases to cover the tracks of the employees involved.

Unauthorized Use at Work

The unauthorized use of a computer system is called **time and resource theft**. A common example is unauthorized use of company-owned computer networks by employees. This may range from doing private consulting or personal finances, or playing video games to unauthorized use of the Internet on company networks. Network monitoring software called *sniffers* is frequently used to monitor network traffic to evaluate network capacity, as well as reveal evidence of improper use.

Software Piracy

Computer programs are valuable property and thus are the subject of theft from computer systems. Unauthorized copying of software or **software piracy** is a major form of software theft because software is intellectual property, which is protected by copyright law and user licensing agreements.

Piracy of Intellectual Property

Software is not the only intellectual property subject to computer-based piracy. Other forms of copyrighted material, such as music, videos, images, articles, books, and other written works are especially vulnerable to copyright infringement, which most courts have deemed illegal. Digitized versions can easily be captured by computer systems and made available for people to access or download at Internet websites, or can be readily disseminated by e-mail as file attachments. The development of peer-to-peer (P2P) networking has made digital versions of copyrighted material even more vulnerable to unauthorized use.

Computer Viruses

One of the most destructive examples of computer crime involves the creation of **computer viruses** or *worms*. They typically enter a computer system through illegal or borrowed copies of software, or through network links to other computer systems. A virus usually copies itself into the operating systems programs, and from there to the hard disk and any inserted floppy disks. Vaccine programs and virus prevention and detection programs are available, but may not work for new types of viruses.

Privacy Issues

The power of information technology to store and retrieve information can have a negative effect on the **right to privacy** of every individual. For example:

◆ Confidential e-mail messages by employees are monitored by many companies

◆ Personal information is being collected about individuals every time they visit a site on the World Wide Web

◆ Confidential information on individuals contained in centralized computer databases by credit bureaus, government agencies, and private business firms has been stolen or misused, resulting in the invasion of privacy, fraud, and other injustices.

◆ Unauthorized use of information can seriously damage the privacy of individuals.

◆ Errors in databases can seriously hurt the credit standing or reputation of individuals.

Some important privacy issues being debated in business and government include the following:

◆ Accessing individuals' private e-mail conversations and computer records, and collecting and sharing information about individuals gained from their visits to Internet websites and newsgroups (violation of privacy).

◆ Always "knowing" where a person is, especially as mobile and paging services become more closely associated with people rather than places (computer monitoring)

◆ Using customer information to market additional business services (computer matching).

◆ Collecting telephone numbers and other personal information to build individual customer profiles (unauthorized personal files).

Privacy on the Internet

The Internet is notorious for giving its users a feeling of anonymity, when in actuality, they are highly visible and open to violations of their privacy. Most of the Internet and its World Wide Web and newsgroups are still a wide open, unsecured, electronic frontier, with no tough rules on what information is personal and private. You can protect your privacy in several ways:

◆ Use encryption to send e-mail (both sender and receiver must have encryption software).

◆ Use anonymous remailers to protect your identity when you add comments in newsgroup postings.

◆ Ask your Internet service provider not to sell your name and personal information to mailing list providers, and other marketers.

◆ Decline to reveal personal data and interest on online service and websites user profiles.

Computer Matching

Computer matching is the use of computers to screen and match data about individual characteristics provided by a variety of computer-based information systems and databases in order to identify individuals for business, government, or other purposes. Unauthorized use or mistakes in the computer matching of personal data can be a threat to privacy. For example, an individual's personal profile may be incorrectly matched with someone else's.

Privacy Laws

In the U.S., the Federal Privacy Act strictly regulates the collection and use of personal data by governmental agencies. The law specifies that individuals have the right to inspect their personal records, make copies, and correct or remove erroneous or misleading information.

The Federal Privacy Act specifies that federal agencies:

- ◆ Must annually disclose the types of personal data files they maintain.
- ◆ Cannot disclose personal information on an individual to any other individual or agency except under certain strict conditions.
- ◆ Must inform individuals of the reasons for requesting personal information from them.
- ◆ Must retain personal data records only if it is "relevant and necessary to accomplish" an agency's legal purpose.
- ◆ Must establish appropriate administrative, technical, and physical safeguards to ensure the security and confidentiality of records.

The U.S. Congress enacted the Electronic Communications Privacy Act and the Computer Fraud and Abuse Act in 1986. These federal **privacy laws** are a major attempt to enforce the privacy of computer-based files and communications. These laws prohibit intercepting data communications messages, stealing or destroying data, or trespassing in federal-related computer systems.

Computer Libel and Censorship

The opposite side of the privacy debate is:

- ◆ The right of people to know about matters others may want to keep private (freedom of information)
- ◆ The right of people to express their opinions about such matters (freedom of speech)
- ◆ The right of people to publish those opinions (freedom of the press).

Some of the biggest battlegrounds in the debate are the bulletin boards, e-mail boxes, and online files of the Internet and public information networks, such as America Online and the Microsoft Network. The weapons being used in this battle include *spamming, flame mail,* libel laws, and censorship.

Spamming - is the indiscriminate sending of unsolicited e-mail messages (spam) to many Internet users. Spamming is the favorite tactic of mass-mailers of unsolicited advertisements, or *junk e-mail.* Cyber criminals to spread computer viruses or infiltrate many computer systems have also used spamming.

Flaming - is the practice of sending extremely critical, derogatory, and often vulgar e-mail messages (flame mail), or newsgroup postings to other users on the Internet or online services. Flaming is especially prevalent on some of the Internet's special interest newsgroups. The Internet is very vulnerable to abuse, as it currently lacks formal policing, and lack of security.

Computer Monitoring

One of the most explosive ethical issues concerning the quality of working conditions in e-business is **computer monitoring**. Computers are being used to monitor the productivity and behavior of employees while they work. Supposedly, computer monitoring is done so employers can collect productivity data about their employees to increase the efficiency and quality of service.

Computer monitoring has been criticized as unethical because:

◆ It is used to monitor individuals, not just work, and is done continually, thus violating workers' privacy and personal freedom.

◆ Is considered an invasion of the privacy of employees, because in many cases, they do not know that they are being monitored, or don't know how the information is being used.

◆ The employee's right of due process may be harmed by the improper use of collected data to make personnel decisions.

◆ It increases the stress on employees who must work under constant electronic surveillance.

◆ It has been blamed for causing health problems among monitored workers.

◆ It has also been blamed for robbing workers of the dignity of their work.

Tools of Security Management

The goal of **security management** is the accuracy, integrity, and safety of all e-business processes and resources. Effective security management can minimize errors, fraud, and losses in the internetworked computer-based systems that interconnect today's e-business enterprises.

Internetworked Security Defense

Security of today's internetworked e-business enterprises is a major management challenge. Vital network links and business flows need to be protected from external attack by cyber criminals or subversion by the criminal or irresponsible acts of insiders. This requires a variety of security tools and defensive measures and a coordinated security management program.

Encryption

Encryption of data has become an important way to protect data and other computer network resources especially on the Internet, intranets, and extranets.

Encryption characteristics include:

◆ Passwords, messages, files, and other data can be transmitted in scrambled form and unscrambled by computer systems for authorized users only.

◆ Encryption involves using special mathematical algorithms, or *keys*, to transform digital data into a scrambled code before they are transmitted, and to decode the data when they are received.

◆ The most widely used encryption method uses a pair of *public* and *private* keys unique to each individual. For example: e-mail could be scrambled and encoded using a unique public key for the recipient that is known to the sender. After the e-mail is transmitted, only the recipient's secret private key could unscramble the message.

◆ Encryption programs are sold as separate products or built into other software used for the encryption process.

◆ There are several competing software encryption standards, but the top two are RSA and PGP.

Firewalls

Another important method for control and security on the Internet and other networks is the use of *firewall* computers and software. A network firewall can be a communications processor, typically a *router*, or a dedicated server, along with firewall software.

Fire wall computers and software characteristics include:

◆ A fire wall serves as a "gatekeeper" computer system that protects a company's intranets and other computer networks from intrusion by serving as a filter and safe transfer point for access to and from the Internet and other networks.

◆ A fire wall computer screens all network traffic for proper passwords and other security codes, and only allows authorized transmissions in and out of the network.

◆ Fire walls have become an essential component of organizations connecting to the Internet, because of its vulnerability and lack of security.

◆ Fire walls can deter, but not completely prevent, unauthorized access (hacking) into computer networks. In some cases, a fire wall may allow access only from trusted locations on the Internet to particular computers inside the fire wall. Or it may allow only "safe" information to pass.

◆ In some cases, it is impossible to distinguish safe use of a particular network service from unsafe use and so all requests must be blocked. The fire wall may then provide substitutes for some network services that perform most of the same functions but are not as vulnerable to penetration.

189

Denial of Service Defenses

The Internet is extremely vulnerable to a variety of assaults by criminal hackers, especially *denial of service* (DOS) attacks. Denial of service assaults via the Internet depend on three layers of networked computer systems, and these are the basic steps e-business companies and other organizations can take to protect their websites form denial of service and other hacking attacks. The organization should protect:

- ◆ The victim's website
- ◆ The victim's Internet service provider (ISP)
- ◆ The sites of "zombie" or slave computers that were commandeered by the cyber criminals.

e-Mail Monitoring

Internet and other online e-mail systems are one of the favorite avenues of attack by hackers for spreading computer viruses or breaking into networked computers. E-mail is also the battleground for attempts by companies to enforce policies against illegal, personal, or damaging messages by employees, and the demands of some employees and others, who see such policies as violations of privacy rights.

Virus Defenses

Many companies are building defences against the spread of viruses by centralizing the distribution and updating of antivirus software, as a responsibility of their IS departments. Other companies are outsourcing the virus protection responsibility to their Internet service providers or to telecommunications or security management companies.

Other Security Measures

A variety of security measures are commonly used to protect e-business systems and networks. These include both hardware and software tools like fault-tolerant computers and security monitors, and security policies and procedures such as passwords and backup files.

Security Codes

Typically, a multilevel *password* system is used for security management.

- ◆ First, an end user logs on to the computer system by entering his or her unique identification code, or user ID. The end user is then asked to enter a password in order to gain access into the system.

◆ Next, to access an individual file, a unique file name must be entered.

Backup Files

Backup files, which are duplicate files of data or programs, are another important security measure.

- ◆ Files can be protected by file retention measures that involve storing copies of files from previous periods.
- ◆ Several generations of files can be kept for control purposes.

Security Monitors

System *security monitors* are programs that monitor the use of computer systems and networks and protect them from unauthorized use, fraud, and destruction.

- ◆ Security monitor programs provide the security measures needed to allow only authorized users to access the networks.
- ◆ Security monitors also control the use of the hardware, software, and data resources of a computer system.
- ◆ Security monitors can be used to monitor the use of computer networks and collect statistics on any attempts at improper use.

Biometric Security

These are security measures provided by computer devices, which measure physical traits that make each individual unique. This includes:

- ◆ Voice verification
- ◆ Fingerprints
- ◆ Hand geometry
- ◆ Signature dynamics
- ◆ Keystroke analysis
- ◆ Retina scanning
- ◆ Face recognition

Computer Failure Controls

A variety of controls are needed to prevent computer failure or to minimize its effects. Computer systems may fail due to:

- Power failure
- Electronic circuitry malfunctions
- Telecommunications network problems
- Hidden programming errors
- Computer operator errors
- Electronic vandalism

The information services department typically takes steps to prevent equipment failure and to minimize its detrimental effects. For example,

- Programs of preventative maintenance of hardware and management of software updates are commonplace
- Using computers equipped with automatic and remote maintenance capabilities
- Establishing standards for electrical supply, air conditioning, humidity control, and fire prevention standards
- Arrange for a backup computer system capability with disaster recovery organizations.
- Scheduling and implementing major hardware or software changes to avoid problems.
- Training and supervision of computer operators.
- Using **fault tolerant** computer systems (*fail-safe* and *fail-soft* capabilities)

Fault Tolerant Systems

Many firms use fault tolerant computer systems that have redundant processors, peripherals, and software that provide a capability to back up components in the event of system failure.

- **Fail-Safe** - Fail-Safe refers to computer systems that continue to operate at the same level of performance after a major failure.
- **Fail-Soft** - Fail-Soft refers to computer systems that continue to operate at a reduced but acceptable level after a system failure.

Disaster Recovery

Hurricanes, earthquakes, fires, floods, criminal and terrorist acts, and human error can all severely damage an organization's computing resources, and thus the health of the organization itself. Many companies, especially online e-commerce retailers and wholesalers, airlines, banks, and Internet service providers, for example, are crippled by losing even a few hours of computing power. That is why it is important for organizations to develop **disaster recovery** procedures and formalize them in a *disaster recovery plan*. It specifies which employees will participate in disaster recovery, and what their duties will be; what hardware, software, and facilities will be used; and the priority of applications that will be processed. Arrangements with other companies for use of alternative facilities as a disaster recovery site and off site storage of an organization's databases are also part of an effective recovery effort.

System Controls and Audits

The development of information system controls and the accomplishment of e-business systems audits are two other types of security management.

Information Systems Controls

Information systems controls are methods and devices that attempt to ensure the accuracy, validity, and propriety of information system activities. Information System (IS) controls must be developed to ensure proper data entry, processing techniques, storage methods, and information output. IS controls are designed to monitor and maintain the quality and security of the input, processing, output, and storage activities of any information system.

Auditing IT Systems

E-business systems should be periodically examined, or audited, by a company's internal auditing staff or external auditors from professional accounting firms. Such audits should review and evaluate whether proper and adequate security measures and management policies have been developed and implemented.

An important objective of e-business system audits is testing the integrity of an application audit trail. An *audit trail* can be defined as the presence of documentation that allows a transaction to be traced through all stages of its information processing. In the past, the audit trail of manual information systems was quite visible and easy to trace; however, computer-based information systems have changed the form of the audit trail.

Depending on the value of the company's information, the CFO may want to authorize funding for careful attention to an audit log of computer activity. An audit log records all network traffic—where it's coming from, where in the network it goes, and what it does. Software can detect and flag suspicious activity. While the log does nothing to prevent what's already happened, it can allow computer forensic experts—be they police officers, consultants, or your own people—to either prevent a repeat of the invasion or to lie in wait for a second attack possibly identifying the invader for subsequent prosecution.

An Incomplete Checklist for a Comprehensive Plan

You may not be able to block every angle of attack, but here are a few steps and points that will help minimize your vulnerability.

◆ Develop a comprehensive plan that touches all parts and functions of your organization and all points of vulnerability.

◆ Evaluate, prioritize and defend information appropriately.

◆ Put up good firewalls between the Internet and the strictly internal part of your network.

◆ Consider a virtual private network for essential lines, such as those carrying fund transfers.

◆ Assume attack will come from those most able to do it, i.e., insiders.

◆ Consider preventing outgoing e-mail from carrying attachments.

◆ Encrypt all data that goes over the internet, especially if it relates to transfers funds.

◆ Ensure physical security of computers, related paper files, floppy disks, backup media, and the like.

◆ Establish and propagate a written policy on computer security.

◆ Educate all employees on how to comply with computer security policy.

◆ Keep and monitor an audit log of network traffic.

◆ Inform employees that the computer is monitored.

◆ Do background checks on all new employees. Know the people who have access to your system.

◆ Have the system vulnerability tested, ideally by a third party.

◆ Ensure password security by using unguessable words. Change passwords and log-ins often.

◆ Use the traditional kinds of checks and balances you use to prevent fraud.

◆ Use antivirus software at all levels of the network. Keep it updated.

◆ Back up all data. Keep the back-up media safe.

Recent Trends in the Computer Security Industry

Since the 9/11 terrorist attacks, security issues remain a high priority not only for government officials, but also for corporate executives concerned about the vulnerability of their computer and communications networks, as well as the safety of their employees and customers.

These concerns have fueled more growth in the security industry. A recent survey by The Conference Board and ASIS International (formerly the American Society for Industrial Security— (www.asisonline.org) found a median increase in security spending of 4% among organizations polled with 7% of respondent companies increasing their security budgets by 50% or more. Some of that increased spending apparently paid for personnel. Forty seven percent of survey respondents reported increases in security staffing levels since 2001. Among financial services companies responding, 62% increased security staff during the last two years while 53% of companies in the digital industries—technology, media, and telecommunications—reported increases.

In particular, there's a demand for managers with recognized security expertise and professional certifications such as the CPP (Certified Protection Professional), PCI (Professional Certified Investigator) or PSP (Physical Security Professional). Federal, state, and local government agencies are among the employers increasingly looking for ways to objectively assess the experience and skills of security professionals—and professional certification is one way to do so.

The growing interest in professional certification is a recent phenomenon. Another recent trend is the collaboration between the physical and IT aspects of security. In the past, the IT security team did its work and the physical security team its work quite separately. Now, companies are taking a much more holistic approach that includes data, computer and information security with the policies, planning and procedures that also apply to physical security. This allows for a much more comprehensive strategy, which is, to some degree, expanding and changing the roles of security personnel, particularly at the senior levels.

It's increasingly important for top security officers to learn to speak the language of the executive suite and understand the financial and strategic consequences of the security function in their organizations. There's a growing need for security executives to increase their business abilities. Security officers are seeing changes in their duties and skill requirements, too. Some of the new procedures require officers to handle more complex security equipment. Training tenants in fire and life safety procedures has also become a more important part of the security role in multistory buildings. If people are properly trained, it can mitigate casualties.

For individuals interested in pursuing careers in the security field, opportunities for entry are plentiful. One can start as a security officer and advance through the ranks into supervisory and management roles. Seasoned IT professionals can also find opportunities in the security arena. Interested individuals should understand the connectivity of various systems, have a comprehensive knowledge of different types of IT systems and network architecture and an understanding of where their particular skills lie. A common mistake people make is believing they are a "Jack-of-all-trades."

People who have been network or email administrators are among the IT professionals that have successfully retooled to pursue careers in IT security. For management executives considering careers in security, "a platform of security understanding that includes protection of proprietary information, protection of facilities and protection of executives is necessary."

Glossary

Audit trails: contain information regarding any additions, deletions, or modifications to the system providing evidence concerning transactions. An effective audit trail allows the data to be retrieved and certified. Audit trails will give information regarding the date and time of the transaction, who processed it and at which terminal.

Biometrics: a technique that identifies people based on their unique physical characteristics or behavioral traits.

Computer Crime: criminal actions accomplished through the use of computer systems, especially with intent to defraud, destroy, or make unauthorized use of computer system resources.

Computer Fraud and Abuse Act: a federal law making it a crime for any unauthorized use (copying, damaging, obtaining database information, etc.) of computer hardware or software across state lines.

Computer security: intended to safeguard software, data, hardware, and personnel.

Computer virus: a program that replicates and spreads by attaching itself to other programs. When the infected program is run, the virus executes an event.

Contingency planning: a strategy to minimize the effect of disturbances and to allow for timely resumption of activities. The aim of contingency planning is to minimize the effects of a disruption on your organizations. A disruption is any security violation, man-made or natural, intentional or accidental, that affects normal operations.

Denial of Service: a process whereby hackers overwhelm a website with requests for service from captive computers.

Digital signature: a digital code that can be attached to an electronically transmitted message that uniquely identifies the sender.

Electronic Data Interchange (EDI) systems: online systems where computers automatically perform transactions such as order processing and generating invoices. EDI is the electronic transfer of business information among trading partners.

Encryption: the process of taking information that exists in some readable form and converting it into a form so that it cannot be understood by others.

eToken: a car key-sized authentication token that plugs into a computer's Universal Serial Bus (USB) port, a standard feature on virtually all PCs and laptops manufactured since 1997.

Expected loss (loss expectancy): loss expectancy = probability of loss *times* amount of loss.

Firewall: a system or group of systems that enforces an access control policy between two networks.

Hacking: (1) obsessive use of a computer or, (2) the unauthorized access and use of computer systems.

Iris recognition technology: involves the use of a camera to capture an image of the iris, the colored portion of the eye.

Kerberos: an authentication system developed at MIT. Kerberos was created as a solution to network security problems carried on by insiders. It is designed to enable two parties to exchange private information across an insecure network connection.

Network configuration (topology): the physical shape of the network in terms of the layout of linking stations. A node refers to a workstation. A bridge is a connection between two similar networks. Network protocols are software implementations providing support for network data transmission.

Network security: security needed for both local area networks (LANs) and wide area networks (WANs).

Orange Book: the real title, Trusted Computer System Evaluation Criteria, is a US government publication. It standardizes security system requirements and defines four broad categories of security for host-based environments: (1) minimal security (least), (2) discretionary protection, (3) mandatory protection, and (4) verified protection (most).

Packet filtering: selectively controlling flow of data packets into and out of a network using a rule set based on the header information contained in the data packet itself.

Proxy server: a machine that answers requests for clients by using the server's own address, the primary purpose being to allow a single IP (internet provider) addresses to be used with several physical hosts or networks.

Router: a computer or dedicated hardware device responsible for determining the path that packets should follow to reach a given destination network host. Bridges and gateways also provide a routing function

Salami slicing: a program designed to siphon off small amounts of money from a large number of transactions, so the quantity taken is not really apparent.

Security administrator: a manager that sets computer security policy, subject to board approval. She also investigates and monitors, advises employees, counsels management, and acts as a technical specialist.

Security Analysis Tool for Auditing Networks (SATAN): a tool to help security administrators identify network security problems.

Smart card: a credit card-sized device that has an embedded microprocessor, a small amount of memory, and an interface that allows it to communicate with a workstation or network.

Spamming: the indiscriminate sending of unsolicited e-mail to many Internet users. Spamming is the favorite tactic of mass-mailers of unsolicited advertisements, or *junk e-mail.*

Super zapping: a method of using a utility "zap" program that can bypass controls to modify programs or data.

Tunneling: technology that enables one network to send its data via another network's connections.

Trade secret: all forms and types of financial, business, scientific, technical, economic or engineering information, provided the owner has taken reasonable measures to keep such information secret and the information derives independent economic value (actual or potential) from not being made public.

Trap door: a technique that allows for breaking into a program code, making it possible to insert additional instructions.

Trojan horse: an illegal program, contained within another program, that "sleeps" until some specific event occurs, then triggers the illegal program to be activated and cause damage.

Worm: a program which replicates itself and penetrates a valid computer system. It may spread within a network, penetrating all connected computers.

Index